Jenkins Essentials

Continuous Integration – setting up the stage for a DevOps culture

Mitesh Soni

BIRMINGHAM - MUMBAI

Jenkins Essentials

First published: July 2015

Production reference: 1220715

Published by Packt Publishing Ltd.
Livery Place
35 Livery Street
Birmingham B3 2PB, UK.

ISBN 978-1-78355-347-1

www.packtpub.com

Table of Contents

1
Exploring Jenkins

"Continuous effort – not strength or intelligence – is the key to unlocking our potential."

– Winston Churchill

Jenkins is an open source application written in Java. It is one of the most popular **continuous integration** (CI) tools used to build and test different kinds of projects. In this chapter, we will have a quick overview of Jenkins, essential features, and its impact on DevOps culture. Before we can start using Jenkins, we need to install it. In this chapter, we have provided a step-by-step guide to install Jenkins. Installing Jenkins is a very easy task and is different from the OS flavors.

We will also learn the basic configuration of Jenkins. We will take a quick tour of some key sections of the Jenkins UI and plugin installations as well. This chapter will also cover the DevOps pipeline and how the rest of the chapters will cover implementing it.

To be precise, we will discuss the following topics in this chapter:

- Introduction to Jenkins and its features
- Installation of Jenkins on Windows and the CentOS operating system
- A jump-start tour of the Jenkins dashboard
- How to change configuration settings in Jenkins
- What is the deployment pipeline

On your mark, get set, go!

Introduction to Jenkins and its features

Let's first understand what continuous integration is. CI is one of the most popular application development practices in recent times. Developers integrate bug fix, new feature development, or innovative functionality in code repository. The CI tool verifies the integration process with an automated build and automated test execution to detect issues with the current source of an application, and provide quick feedback.

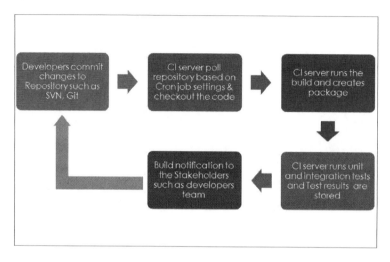

Jenkins is a simple, extensible, and user-friendly open source tool that provides CI services for application development. Jenkins supports SCM tools such as StarTeam, Subversion, CVS, Git, AccuRev and so on. Jenkins can build Freestyle, Apache Ant, and Apache Maven-based projects.

The concept of plugins makes Jenkins more attractive, easy to learn, and easy to use. There are various categories of plugins available such as Source code management, Slave launchers and controllers, Build triggers, Build tools, Build notifies, Build reports, other post-build actions, External site/tool integrations, UI plugins, Authentication and user management, Android development, iOS development, .NET development, Ruby development, Library plugins, and so on.

Jenkins defines interfaces or abstract classes that model a facet of a build system. Interfaces or abstract classes define an agreement on what needs to be implemented; Jenkins uses plugins to extend those implementations.

What is the deployment pipeline?

The application development life cycle is a traditionally lengthy and a manual process. In addition, it requires effective collaboration between development and operations teams. The deployment pipeline is a demonstration of automation involved in the application development life cycle containing the automated build execution and test execution, notification to the stakeholder, and deployment in different runtime environments. Effectively, the deployment pipeline is a combination of CI and continuous delivery, and hence is a part of DevOps practices. The following diagram depicts the deployment pipeline process:

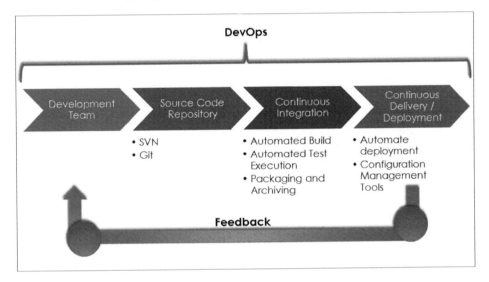

Members of the development team check code into a source code repository. CI products such as Jenkins are configured to poll changes from the code repository. Changes in the repository are downloaded to the local workspace and Jenkins triggers an automated build process, which is assisted by Ant or Maven. Automated test execution or unit testing, static code analysis, reporting, and notification of successful or failed build process are also part of the CI process.

Once the build is successful, it can be deployed to different runtime environments such as testing, preproduction, production, and so on. Deploying a war file in terms of the JEE application is normally the final stage in the deployment pipeline.

One of the biggest benefits of the deployment pipeline is the faster feedback cycle. Identification of issues in the application at early stages and no dependencies on manual efforts make this entire end-to-end process more effective.

In the next chapters, we will see how Jenkins can be used for implementing CI practices in modernizing IT.

 To read more, visit `http://martinfowler.com/bliki/DeploymentPipeline.html` and `http://www.informit.com/articles/article.aspx?p=1621865&seqNum=2`.

Self-test questions

Q1. What is Jenkins?

1. A continuous integration product
2. A continuous delivery product

Q2. What makes Jenkins extensible?

1. Plugins
2. Open Source Distribution

Q3. Which command is used to run the Jenkins installation file in the `war` format?

1. java –jar `Jenkins.war`
2. java –j `Jenkins.war`

Q4. How do we get system information on the Jenkins dashboard?

1. Visit `http://<ip_address>:8080/manage`
2. Visit `http://<ip_address>:8080/systeminfo`

Q5. How do we change global settings for configuration on the Jenkins dashboard?

1. Click on the **Manage Jenkins** link on the dashboard
2. Click on the **Credentials** link on the dashboard

Q6. What is the deployment pipeline?

1. Continuous Integration Practices
2. Continuous Delivery Practices
3. Demonstration of automation involved in the application development life cycle
4. None of the above

Q7. Explain the benefits of the deployment pipeline?

1. Faster feedback cycle

2. Identification of issues in an application at early stages

3. No dependencies on manual efforts

4. All of the above

Summary

Congratulations! We reached the end of this chapter and hence we have Jenkins installed on our physical or virtual machine, and you are ready to go to the next chapter. Till now, we covered the basics of CI and the introduction to Jenkins and its features. We completed the installation of Jenkins on Windows and CentOS platforms. We also completed a quick tour of features available in Jenkins's dashboard. In addition to this, we discussed the deployment pipeline and its importance in CI.

Now that we are able to use our CI server, Jenkins, we can begin creating a job and verify how Jenkins works.

2
Installation and Configuration of Code Repository and Build Tools

"Life is really simple, but we insist on making it complicated"

– Confucius

We looked at the deployment pipeline in the last chapter in which the source code repository and automated build form a significant part. SVN, Git, CVS, and StarTeam are some of the popular code repositories that manage changes to code, artifacts, or documents, while Ant and Maven are popular build automation tools for Java applications.

This chapter describes in detail how to prepare a runtime environment for life cycle management with a Java application and configure it with Jenkins. It will cover how to integrate Eclipse and code repositories such as SVN to create a base for continuous integration. The following is the list of topics covered in this chapter:

- Overview of a build in Jenkins and its requirements
- Installing Java and configuring environment variables
- SVN installation, configuration, and operations on CentOS and Windows
- Installing Ant
- Configuring Ant, Maven, and JDK in Jenkins
- Integrating Eclipse with code repositories
- Installing and configuring Git
- Creating a new build job in Jenkins with Git

An overview of a build in Jenkins and its requirements

To explain continuous integration, we are going to use a code repository installed on a physical machine or laptop while Jenkins is installed on a virtual machine, as suggested in different ways in *Chapter 1, Exploring Jenkins*. The following figure depicts the setup of the runtime environment:

We saw in *Chapter 1, Exploring Jenkins,* that the **Manage Jenkins** link on the dashboard is used to configure the system. Click on the **Configure System** link to configure Java, Ant, Maven, and other third-party product-related information. We can create a virtual machine with Virtual box or the VMware workstation. We need to install all required software to provide a runtime environment for continuous integration. We assume that Java is already installed in the system.

Installing Java and configuring environment variables

If Java is not already installed in the system then you can install it as follows:

Find the Java related packages available in CentOS repository and locate the appropriate package to install.

```
[root@localhost ~]# yum search java
Loaded plugins: fastestmirror, refresh-packagekit, security
```

.

.

```
ant-javamail.x86_64 : Optional javamail tasks for ant
eclipse-mylyn-java.x86_64 : Mylyn Bridge:  Java Development
```

.

.

```
java-1.5.0-gcj.x86_64 : JPackage runtime compatibility layer for GCJ
java-1.5.0-gcj-devel.x86_64 : JPackage development compatibility layer
for GCJ
java-1.5.0-gcj-javadoc.x86_64 : API documentation for libgcj
java-1.6.0-openjdk.x86_64 : OpenJDK Runtime Environment
java-1.6.0-openjdk-devel.x86_64 : OpenJDK Development Environment
java-1.6.0-openjdk-javadoc.x86_64 : OpenJDK API Documentation
java-1.7.0-openjdk.x86_64 : OpenJDK Runtime Environment
jcommon-serializer.x86_64 : JFree Java General Serialization Framework
```

.

.

```
Install the identified package java-1.7.0-openjdk.x86_64
[root@localhost ~]# yum install java-1.7.0-openjdk.x86_64
Loaded plugins: fastestmirror, refresh-packagekit, security
No such command: in. Please use /usr/bin/yum -help
```

Now install Java package available in the local repositories by executing yum
install command as follows:

```
[root@localhost ~]# yum install java-1.7.0-openjdk.x86_64
Loaded plugins: fastestmirror, refresh-packagekit, security
Loading mirror speeds from cached hostfile
Setting up Install Process
Resolving Dependencies
--> Running transaction check
---> Package java-1.7.0-openjdk.x86_64 1:1.7.0.3-2.1.el6.7 will be
installed
--> Finished Dependency Resolution


Dependencies Resolved
```

.

.

```
Install         1 Package(s)


Total download size: 25 M

Installed size: 89 M

Is this ok [y/N]: y

Downloading Packages:

java-1.7.0-openjdk-1.7.0.3-2.1.el6.7.x86_64.rpm
|  25 MB       00:00

Running rpm_check_debug

Running Transaction Test

Transaction Test Succeeded

Running Transaction

  Installing : 1:java-1.7.0-openjdk-1.7.0.3-2.1.el6.7.x86_64
1/1

  Verifying  : 1:java-1.7.0-openjdk-1.7.0.3-2.1.el6.7.x86_64
1/1


Installed:

  java-1.7.0-openjdk.x86_64 1:1.7.0.3-2.1.el6.7

Complete!
```

Java is installed successfully from the local repository.

Configure environment variables

The following are the steps to configure the environment variables:

1. Set JAVA_HOME and JRE_HOME variables

2. Go to /root

3. Press *Ctrl* + *H* to list hidden files

4. Find .bash_profile and edit it by appending the Java path, as shown in the following screenshot:

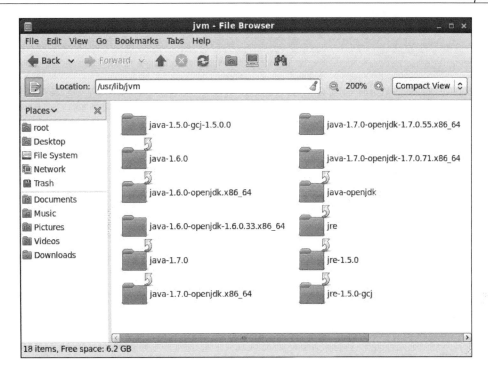

Installing, configuring, and operating SVN on CentOS and Windows

Install SVN from the local repository on CentOS.

Installing SVN on CentOS

To install SVN on a CentOS machine, execute the yum install mod_dav_svn subversion command as follows:

```
[root@localhost ~]# yum install mod_dav_svn subversion
Loaded plugins: fastestmirror, refresh-packagekit, security
Loading mirror speeds from cached hostfile
Setting up Install Process
Resolving Dependencies
--> Running transaction check
---> Package mod_dav_svn.x86_64 0:1.6.11-7.el6 will be installed
```

```
---> Package subversion.x86_64 0:1.6.11-7.el6 will be installed
--> Processing Dependency: perl(URI) >= 1.17 for package:
subversion-1.6.11-7.el6.x86_64
--> Running transaction check
---> Package perl-URI.noarch 0:1.40-2.el6 will be installed
--> Finished Dependency Resolution


Dependencies Resolved

.

.

Installed:
  mod_dav_svn.x86_64 0:1.6.11-7.el6
subversion.x86_64 0:1.6.11-7.el6


Dependency Installed:
  perl-URI.noarch 0:1.40-2.el6
Complete!
[root@localhost ~]#
```

Configuring SVN

Create the password file using the htpasswd command. Initially use the -cm arguments. This creates the file and also encrypts the password with MD5. If you need to add users, make sure you simply use the -m flag, and not the –c, after the initial creation.

```
[root@localhost conf.d]# htpasswd -cm /etc/svn-auth-conf yourusername
New password:
Re-type new password:
Adding password for user yourusername
[root@localhost conf.d]#


[root@localhost conf.d]# htpasswd -cm /etc/svn-auth-conf mitesh
New password:
Re-type new password:
Adding password for user mitesh
[root@localhost conf.d]#
```

Now configure SVN in Apache to integrate both. Edit `/etc/httpd/conf.d/` `subversion.conf`. The location is what Apache will pass in the URL bar.

```
LoadModule dav_svn_module       modules/mod_dav_svn.so
LoadModule authz_svn_module     modules/mod_authz_svn.so


#
# Example configuration to enable HTTP access for a directory
# containing Subversion repositories, "/var/www/svn".  Each repository
# must be both:
#
#   a) readable and writable by the 'apache' user, and
#
#   b) labelled with the 'httpd_sys_content_t' context if using
#   SELinux
#


#
# To create a new repository "http://localhost/repos/stuff" using
# this configuration, run as root:
#
#   # cd /var/www/svn
#   # svnadmin create stuff
#   # chown -R apache.apache stuff
#   # chcon -R -t httpd_sys_content_t stuff
#


<Location />
   DAV svn
   SVNParentPath /var/www/svn/
#
#   # Limit write permission to list of valid users.
#   <LimitExcept GET PROPFIND OPTIONS REPORT>
#       # Require SSL connection for password protection.
#       # SSLRequireSSL
#
```

```
    AuthType Basic
       SVNListParentPath on
    AuthName "Subversion repos"
    AuthUserFile /etc/svn-auth-conf
    Require valid-user
#    </LimitExcept>
</Location>
```

Now all configurations are completed. Let's perform operations on SVN.

SVN operations

Create the actual repository to perform SVN operations on the CentOS virtual machine.

```
[root@localhost ~] cd /var/www/ -- Or wherever you placed your path above
[root@localhost ~] mkdir svn
[root@localhost ~] cd svn
[root@localhost ~] svnadmin create repos
[root@localhost ~] chown -R apache:apache repos
[root@localhost ~] service httpd restart
```

Import a directory into SVN

Create a sample folder structure to test SVN operations. Create the mytestproj directory with sub-directories named main, configurations, and resources. Create sample files in each sub-directory.

```
[root@localhost mytestproj]# svn import /tmp/mytestproj/ file:///var/www/
svn/repos/mytestproj -m "Initial repository layout for mytestproj"
Adding          /tmp/mytestproj/main
Adding          /tmp/mytestproj/main/mainfile1.cfg
Adding          /tmp/mytestproj/configurations
Adding          /tmp/mytestproj/configurations/testconf1.cfg
Adding          /tmp/mytestproj/resources
Adding          /tmp/mytestproj/resources/testresources1.cfg
Committed revision 1.
```

Verify the repository from a web browser: http://localhost/repos.

Check out from SVN

To check out source code from the repository, perform the following operations:

1. Start `httpd` service.

```
[root@localhost testmit]# service httpd restart
Stopping httpd:
[  OK  ]
Starting httpd: httpd: Could not reliably determine the server's
fully qualified domain name, using localhost.localdomain for
ServerName
[  OK  ]
```

2. Check out the source code.

```
[root@localhost testmit]# svn co http://localhost/repos/mytestproj
Authentication realm: <http://localhost:80> Subversion repos
Password for 'root':
Authentication realm: <http://localhost:80> Subversion repos
Username: mitesh
Password for 'mitesh':xxxxxxxxx


-----------------------------------------------------------------
-----
ATTENTION!  Your password for authentication realm:

   <http://localhost:80> Subversion repos


can only be stored to disk unencrypted! You are advised to
configure your system so that Subversion can store passwords
encrypted, if possible. See the documentation for details.
```

3. You can avoid future appearances of this warning by setting the value of the `store-plaintext-passwords` option to either `yes` or `no` in `/root/.subversion/servers`.

```
-----------------------------------------------------------------
-----
Store password unencrypted (yes/no)? no
A    mytestproj/main
A    mytestproj/main/mainfile1.cfg
A    mytestproj/configurations
```

```
A      mytestproj/configurations/testconf1.cfg

A      mytestproj/options

A      mytestproj/options/testopts1.cfg

Checked out revision 1.
```

VisualSVN Server on Windows

1. Download the VisualSVN server from: `https://www.visualsvn.com/server/download/`. It allows you to install and manage a fully-functional Subversion server with Windows.

2. Execute `VisualSVN-Server-x.x.x-x64.msi` and follow the wizard to install VisualSVN Server.

3. Open VisualSVN Server Manager.

4. Create a new repository, `JenkinsTest`.

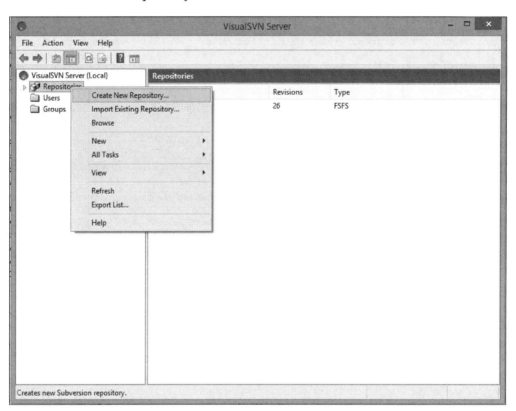

5. Select the regular subversion repository and click on **Next >**.

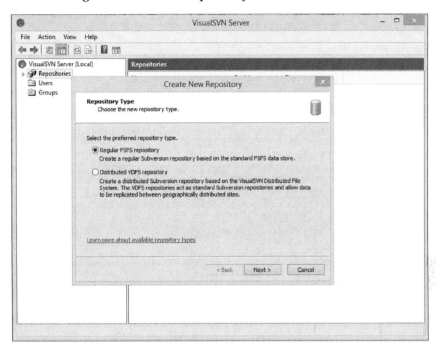

6. Provide the **Repository Name** and click on **Next >**.

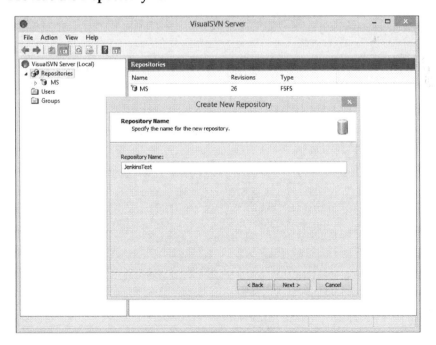

7. Select **Single-project repository** and click on **>**.

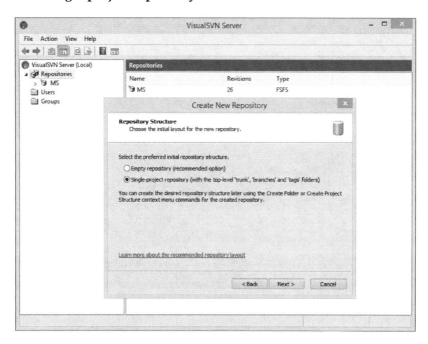

8. Select the Repository Access Permissions based on your requirements and click on **Create**.

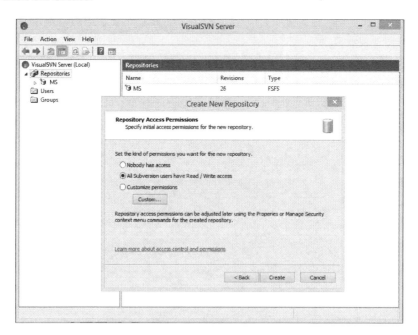

9. Review the created repository details and click on **Finish**.

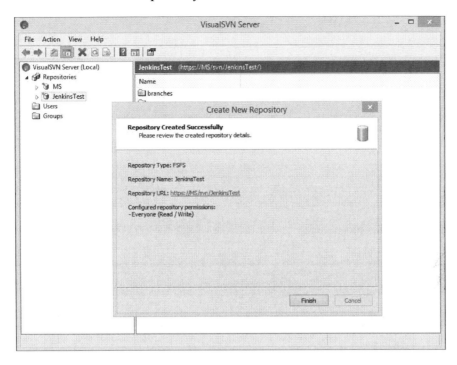

10. Verify the newly created repository in VisualSVN Server Manager.

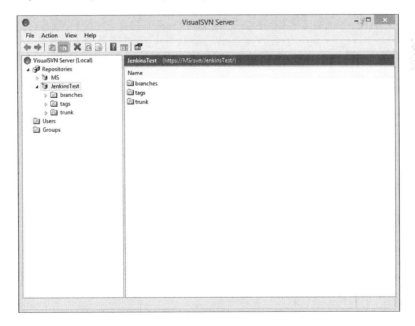

11. Verify the repository location in the browser, as shown in the following screenshot:

12. Now install SVN client from: `http://sourceforge.net/projects/tortoisesvn/`, to perform SVN operations.

Let's create a sample JEE project in Eclipse to illustrate SVN and Eclipse integration.

1. Open Eclipse, go to the **File** menu and click on **Dynamic Web Project**.

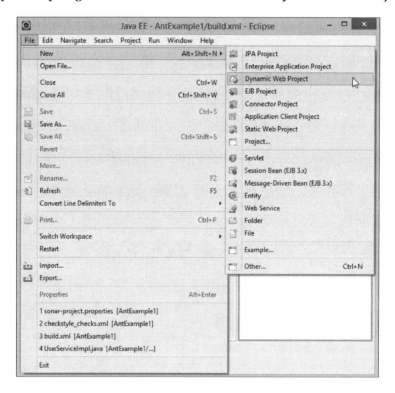

2. It will open a dialog box to create a **New Dynamic Web Project**.

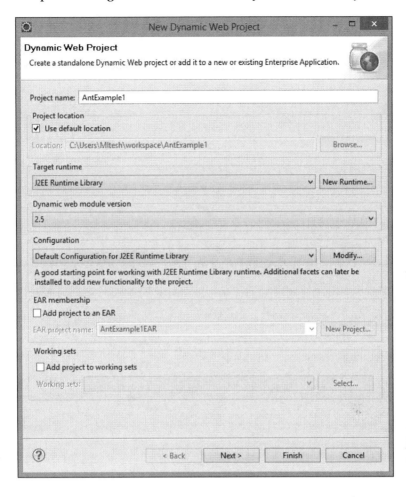

3. Create the source files and a `build` file for a simple project.

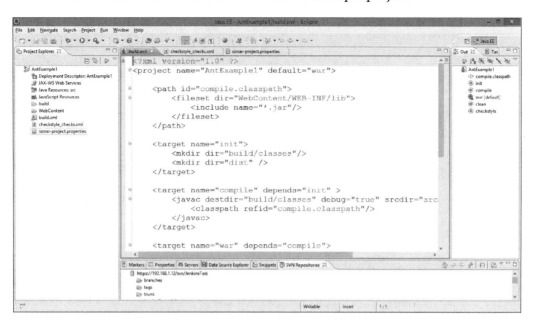

4. Go to **Application Directory**, right-click on it, select **TortoiseSVN**, and select **Import** from the sub-menu.

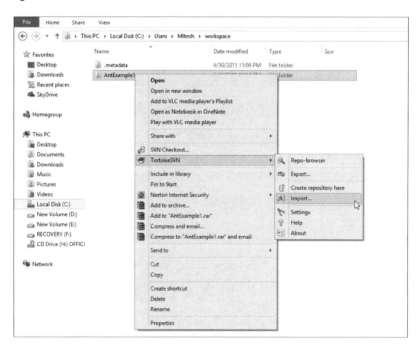

5. Enter the repository URL and click on **OK**.

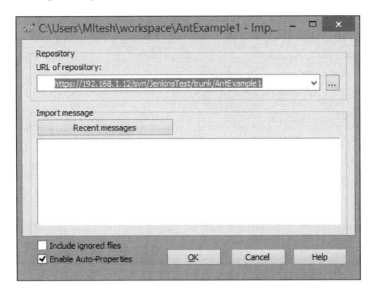

6. It will add all files from the application to SVN, as shown in the following screenshot.

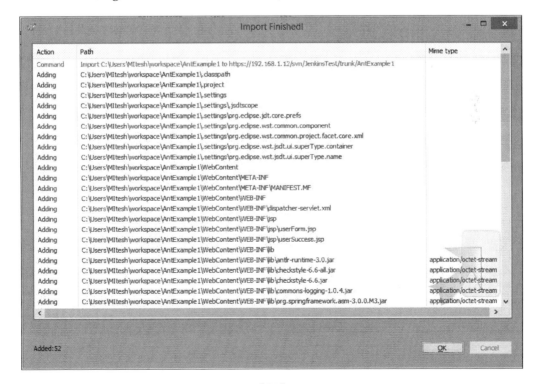

7. Verify the import by visiting the SVN repository in a browser as shown:

Integrating Eclipse with code repositories

1. Open Eclipse IDE, go to the **Help** menu and click on **Install New Software**.

2. Add the repository by adding this URL: `http://subclipse.tigris.org/update_1.10.x`, then select all packages and click on **Next >**.

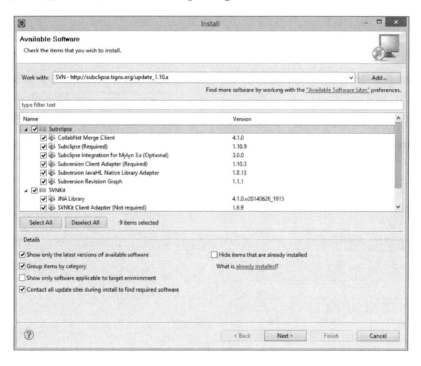

3. Review the items to be installed and the Review Licenses in the wizard. Accept the terms of agreement and click on **Finish**.

4. Restart Eclipse. Go to the **Window** menu, select **Show View**, click on **Other**, and find the SVN and SVN repositories.

5. In the SVN repositories area, right-click and select **New**; select **Repository Location...** from the sub-menu.

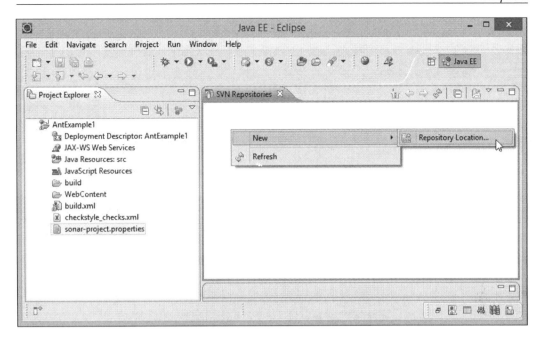

6. Add a new SVN Repository in Eclipse with this URL:
    `https://<Ip address/ localhost / hostname>/svn/JenkinsTest/.`

7. Click on **Finish**.

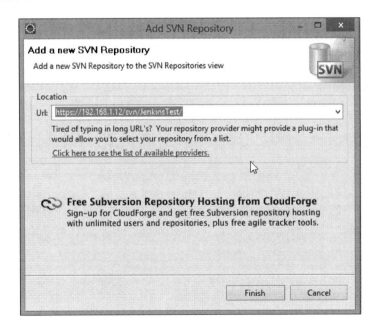

8. Verify the SVN repository.

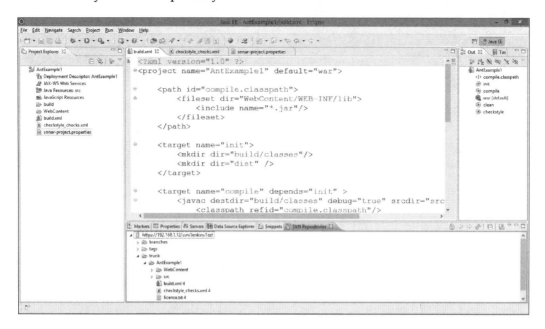

Try to integrate SVN, installed on CentOS, with Eclipse IDE, as practice.

Installing and configuring Ant

1. Download the Ant distribution from: `https://ant.apache.org/bindownload.cgi` and unzip it.

2. Set the ANT_HOME and JAVA_HOME environment variables.

There is an option available in Jenkins to install Ant or Maven automatically. We will study this in the *Configuring Ant, Maven, and JDK in Jenkins* section.

Installing Maven

Download the Maven binary ZIP file from `https://maven.apache.org/download.cgi` and extract it to the local system where Jenkins is installed.

Configuring Ant, Maven, and JDK in Jenkins

1. Open the Jenkins dashboard in your browser with this URL: `http://<ip_address>:8080/configure`. Go to the **Manage Jenkins** section and click on **Configure System**.

2. Configure Java, based on the installation shown in the following screenshot:

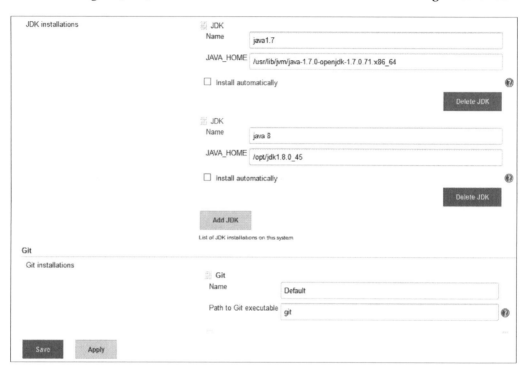

3. Configure or install Ant automatically on the same page. Configure Maven as well.

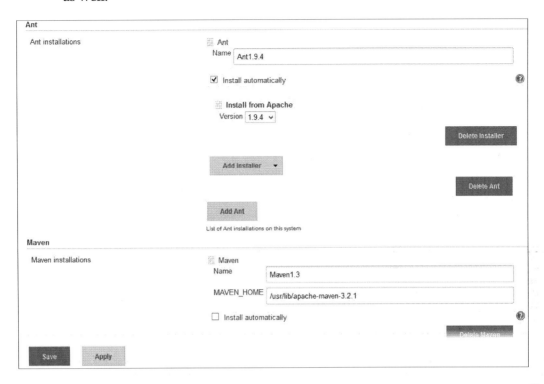

Installing and configuring Git

Git is a free and open source distributed version control system. In this section, we will try to install and configure Git.

1. Open the terminal in the CentOS-based system and execute the command `yum install git` in the terminal.

2. Once it is successfully installed, verify the version with the command `git --version`.

3. Provide information about the user with the `git config` command so that `commit` messages will be generated with the correct information attached.

4. Provide the name and e-mail address to embed into commits.

5. To create a workspace environment, create a directory called `git` in the home directory and then create a subdirectory inside of that called `development`.

   Use `mkdir -p ~/git/development ; cd ~/git/development` in the terminal.

6. Copy the `AntExample1` directory into the `development` folder.

7. Convert an existing project into a workspace environment by using the `git init` command.

8. Once the repository is initialized, add files and folders.

```
root@localhost:~/git/development/AntExample1                  _ □ ×

File  Edit  View  Search  Terminal  Tabs  Help

root@localhost:~/git/development/AntExa...  ✕  root@localhost:/usr              ✕

[root@localhost Desktop]# git --version
git version 1.7.1
[root@localhost Desktop]# git config --global user.name "Mitesh"
[root@localhost Desktop]# git config --global user.email "         @gmail.co
m"
[root@localhost Desktop]# git config --list
user.name=Mitesh
user.email=          @gmail.com
core.repositoryformatversion=0
core.filemode=true
core.bare=false
core.logallrefupdates=true
[root@localhost Desktop]# mkdir -p ~/git/development ; cd ~/git/development
[root@localhost development]# cd AntExample1/
[root@localhost AntExample1]# git init
Initialized empty Git repository in /root/git/development/AntExample1/.git/
[root@localhost AntExample1]# git add .
[root@localhost AntExample1]#
```

9. Commit by executing `git commit -m "Initial Commit" -a`.

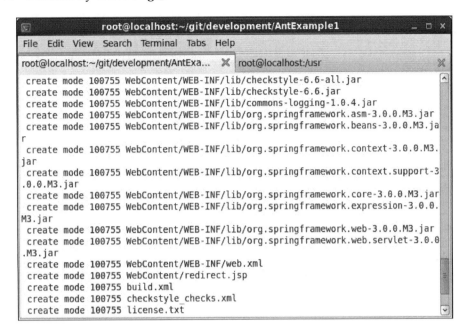

10. Verify the Git repository

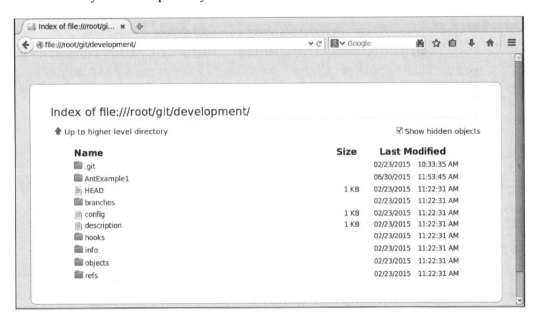

11. Verify the project in the Git repository.

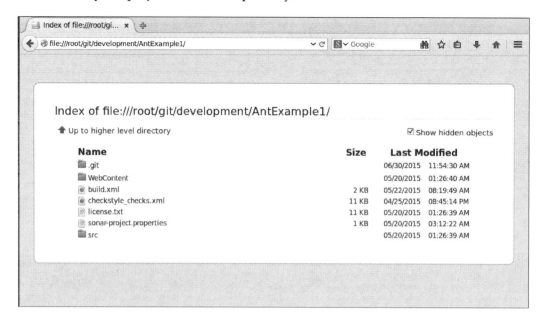

Creating a new build job in Jenkins with Git

1. On the Jenkins dashboard, click on **Manage Jenkins** and select **Manage Plugins**. Click on the **Available** tab and write `github` plugin in the search box.

2. Click the checkbox and click on the button, **Download now and install after restart**.

3. Restart Jenkins.

4. Create a new **Freestyle project**. Provide **Item name** and click on **OK**.

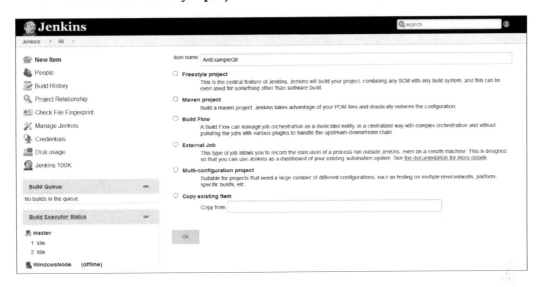

5. Configure **Git** in the **Source Code Management** section.

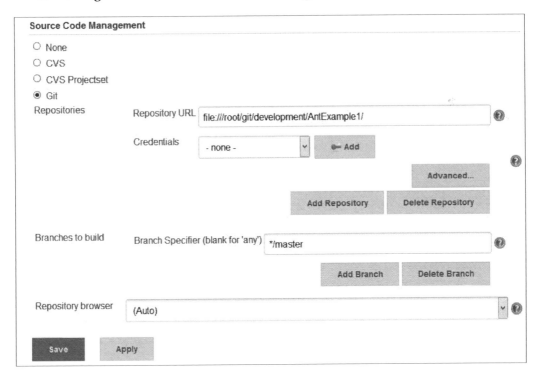

6. Add the **Invoke Ant** build step by clicking on **Add build step**.

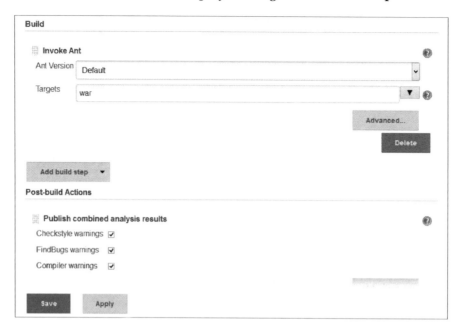

7. Execute the build.

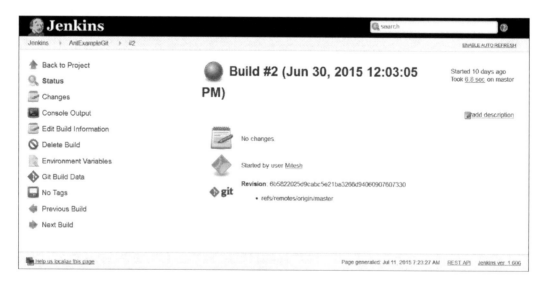

8. Click on **Console Output** to see the progress of the build.

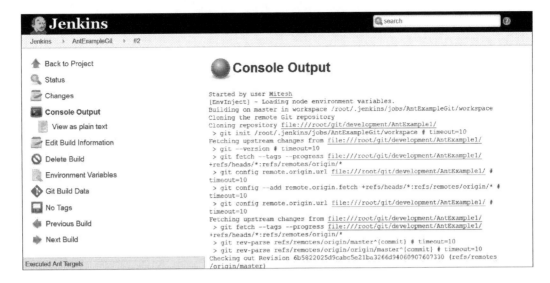

9. Once the build has succeeded, verify **Workspace** in the build job.

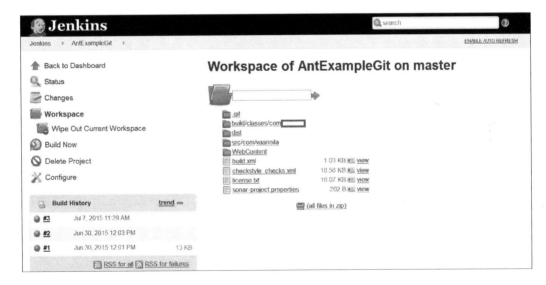

10. Done!

Self-test questions

Q1. Where to set the `JAVA_HOME` and `JRE_HOME` environment variables?

1. `/root/ .bash_profile`
2. `/root/ .env_profile`
3. `/root/ .bash_variables`
4. `/root/ .env_variables`

Q2. Which are valid SVN operations?

1. `svn import /tmp/mytestproj/`
2. `svn co http://localhost/repos/mytestproj`
3. Both the above

Q3. Where do you configure Java and Ant in Jenkins?

1. Go to the **Manage Jenkins** section and click on **Configure System**
2. Go to the **Manage Jenkins** section and click on **Global Configuration**

Summary

Hooray! We have reached the end of this chapter. We have covered how to prepare an environment for continuous integration by setting up a local CentOS repository, installing code repositories such as SVN on CentOS and Windows, and build tool Ant. We have also seen detailed instructions on how to configure repositories and build tools in Jenkins. Finally, we have covered how to integrate the Integrated Development Environment with code repositories so that efficient development and ease of `commit` operations can take place to facilitate the deployment pipeline process.

3
Integration of Jenkins, SVN, and Build Tools

"The barrier to change is not too little caring; it is too much complexity"

– Bill Gates

We have seen how to set up an environment to use Jenkins for continuous integration, and we have also configured build tools in Jenkins. The integration of Eclipse with SVN will help developers to easily perform operations on repositories.

Now we are ready to create our first build job for continuous integration. This chapter describes in detail how to create and configure build jobs for Java applications using build tools such as Ant and Maven; how to run build jobs, unit test cases. It covers all aspects of running a build to create a distribution file or war file for deployment, as well as a Dashboard View plugin to provide a customized display of build jobs and test results based on preferences. The following are the main points which are covered in this chapter:

- Creating and configuring a build job for a Java application with Ant
- Creating and configuring a build job for a Java application with Maven
- Build execution with test cases

Creating and configuring a build job for a Java application with Ant

Before creating and configuring a build job for a Java application, we will install a Dashboard View plugin to better manage builds, and display the results of builds and tests. We have already seen how to create a basic job in *Chapter 2, Installation and Configuration of Code Repository and Build Tools*.

Dashboard View Plugin

This plugin presents a new view that provides a portal-like view for Jenkins build jobs. Download it from `https://wiki.jenkins-ci.org/display/JENKINS/Dashboard+View`. It is good for showing results and trends. In addition, it also allows the user to arrange display items in an effective manner. On the Jenkins dashboard, go to the **Manage Jenkins** link and click on **Manage Plugins** and install the Dashboard View plugin. Verify the installation by clicking on the **Installed** tab.

On the Jenkins dashboard, click on the plus button to create a new view. Provide a **View name** and select the type of view; in our case **Dashboard,** then click on **OK**.

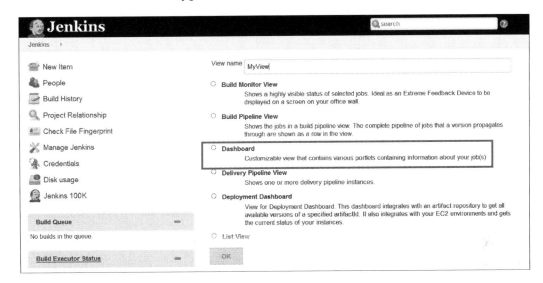

Provide a **Name** and select **Jobs** that need to be included in the view, as shown in the following screenshot:

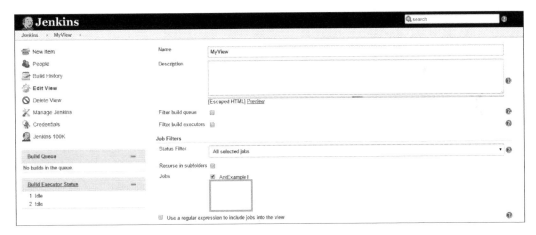

In the View configuration, click on **Add Dashboard Portlet to right column**, and select **Test Statistics Grid**. Add **Test Statistics Chart**. This will display test results in the form of statistics and chart representations of test results.

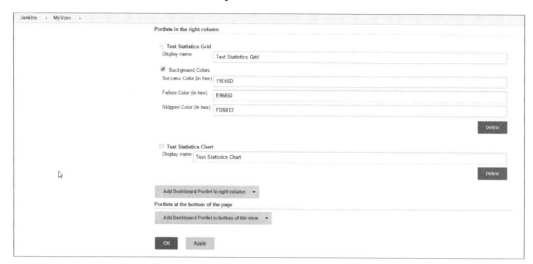

Creating and configuring a build job for a Java application

Click on **New Item** on the dashboard to create a new build for a Java application which uses Ant as a build tool. Enter **Item name**, and select **Freestyle project**. Click **OK**.

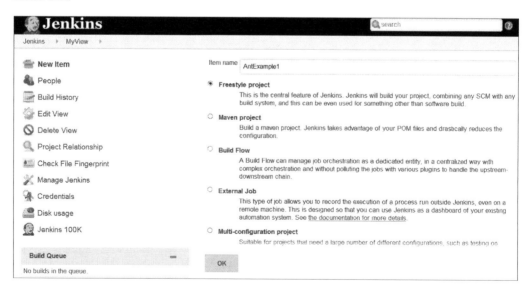

It will open the configuration for a new build job. In **Source Code Management**, select **Subversion**. Provide the **Repository URL** and **Credentials**. In *Chapter 2, Installation and Configuration of Code Repository and Build Tools*, we installed Subversion and also added the source code to SVN.

Provide the URL you use in your browser to access the source code repository.

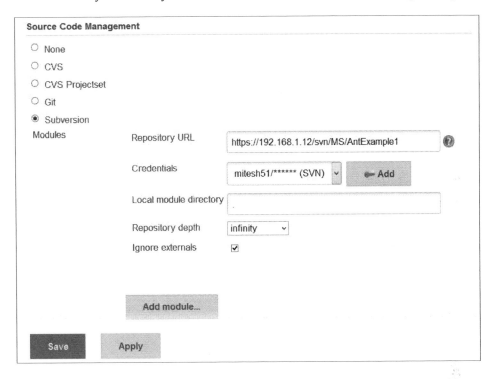

If **Credentials** are not available in the box, click on the **Add** button. Provide **Scope**, **Username**, **Password**, and **Description**, and click on **Add** to make it available on the list box available in the build job configuration. **Scope** determines where credentials can be used. For example system scope restricts credential usage to the object with which the credential is associated. It provides better confidentiality than global scope. Global scope credentials are available to the object with which the credential is associated and all objects that are children of that object.

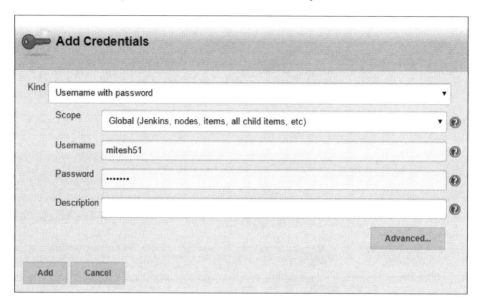

In the build job configuration, go to the **Build Triggers** section and select the **Poll SCM** radio button. Provide the schedule detail in the * * * * * form, as shown in the following figure. It will poll the repository every minute to verify changes committed into the repository by developers.

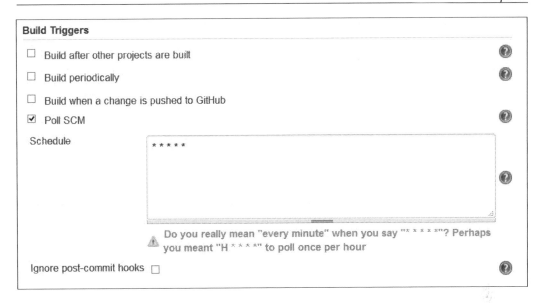

The **Schedule** field follows cron syntax, MINUTE HOUR Day Of the Month MONTH Day Of the Week.

For example, H * * * * to poll once per hour, H/15 * * * * to poll every fifteen minutes.

Once **Build Triggers** and **Source Code Management** configurations are completed, we need to provide build tool-related details, so Jenkins can use them to execute once the build is triggered. Click on the **Add build step** and select **Invoke Ant**. From the drop-down menu, select Ant, configured in *Chapter 2, Installation and Configuration of Code Repository and Build Tools* and provide **Targets** with the name you want to execute from the build.

Click on the **Apply** and **Save** buttons to finalize the configuration. Click on the **Build Now** button on the Jenkins dashboard. It will check out all the latest available code in the source code repository against the local workspace on the machine where Jenkins is installed, as shown in the following figure. In the **build history** section of a specific job, click on **build number**, and then click on **Console Output**.

Once the checkout process is completed, the build file execution, based on the targets, will start, and the build execution will be successful if all dependencies and files required for the build execution are available in the local workspace, as shown in the following figure:

```
Buildfile: /root/.jenkins/jobs/AntExample1/workspace/build.xml

init:
    [mkdir] Created dir: /root/.jenkins/jobs/AntExample1/workspace/build/classes
    [mkdir] Created dir: /root/.jenkins/jobs/AntExample1/workspace/dist

compile:
    [javac] /root/.jenkins/jobs/AntExample1/workspace/build.xml:16: warning:
'includeantruntime' was not set, defaulting to build.sysclasspath=last; set to
false for repeatable builds
    [javac] Compiling 4 source files to /root/.jenkins/jobs/AntExample1/workspace
/build/classes
    [javac] Note: /root/.jenkins/jobs/AntExample1/workspace/src/com/vaannila
/web/UserController.java uses or overrides a deprecated API.
    [javac] Note: Recompile with -Xlint:deprecation for details.

war:
    [war] Building war: /root/.jenkins/jobs/AntExample1/workspace
/dist/AntExample.war

BUILD SUCCESSFUL
Total time: 5 seconds
Started calculate disk usage of build
Finished Calculation of disk usage of build in 0 seconds
Started calculate disk usage of workspace
Finished Calculation of disk usage of workspace in 0 seconds
Finished: SUCCESS
```

To verify the local workspace, go to the view you created, select **build job** and then
click on **Workspace**. Verify that all files and folders are available, as provided by the
source code repository.

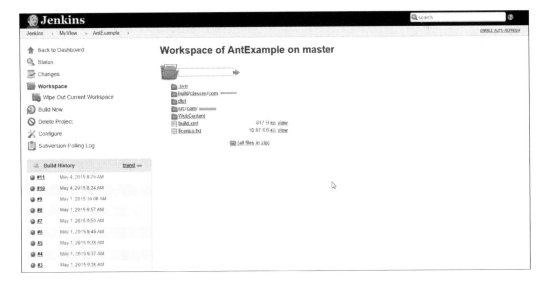

Creating and configuring a build job for a Java application with Maven

Click on **New Item** on the dashboard to create a new build for a Java application which uses Maven as a build tool. Enter the **Item name** and select **Maven project** from the list.

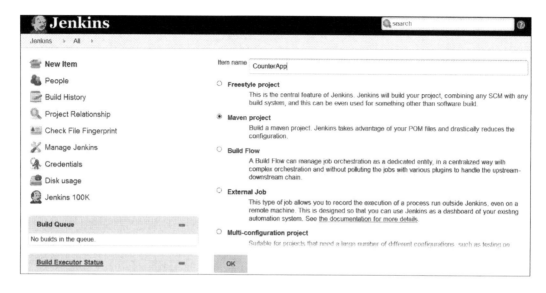

It will open the configuration for the new build job. In **Source Code Management**, select **Subversion**. Provide **Repository URL** and **Credentials**. In *Chapter 2, Installation and Configuration of Code Repository and Build Tools* we installed **Subversion**, and added the source code to SVN.

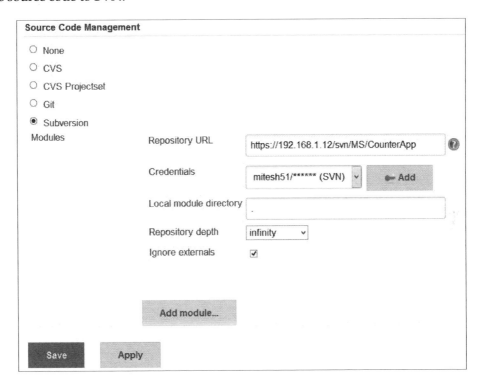

In the build job configuration, go to the **Build Triggers** section and select the **Poll SCM** radio button. Provide the schedule detail in * * * * * form, as shown in following figure. It will poll the repository every minute to verify changes committed into the repository by developers. Add the Maven build step. Provide the name of the build file; by default it is pom.xml. Provide **Goals and Options** and, if you keep it empty, then it will execute the default goal.

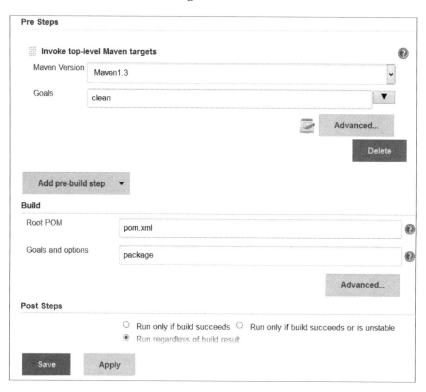

Click on **Build Now** to execute the build job or commit the updated code to the repository, and the build will be executed automatically based on our configuration in **Build Triggers**.

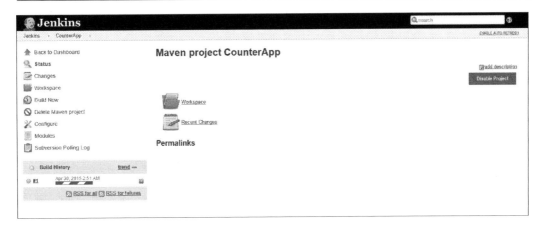

It will check out all the latest available code in the source code repository against the local workspace on the machine where Jenkins is installed, as shown in the following figure.

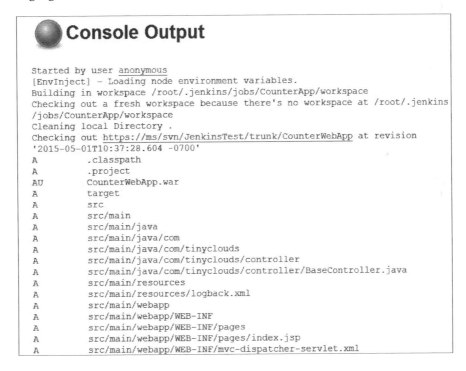

Once the checkout process is completed, the build file execution based on the goals will start, and the build execution will be successful if all dependencies and files required for the build execution are available in the local workspace, as shown in the following figure.

```
[INFO] Installing /root/.jenkins/jobs/CounterApp/workspace/target
/CounterWebApp.war to /root/.m2/repository/com/tinyclouds/CounterWebApp
/1.0-SNAPSHOT/CounterWebApp-1.0-SNAPSHOT.war
[INFO] Installing /root/.jenkins/jobs/CounterApp/workspace/pom.xml to /root/.m2
/repository/com/tinyclouds/CounterWebApp/1.0-SNAPSHOT/CounterWebApp-
1.0-SNAPSHOT.pom
[INFO] ------------------------------------------------------------
[INFO] BUILD SUCCESS
[INFO] ------------------------------------------------------------
[INFO] Total time: 6.307 s
[INFO] Finished at: 2015-05-01T10:37:41-08:00
[INFO] Final Memory: 15M/36M
[INFO] ------------------------------------------------------------
[JENKINS] Archiving /root/.jenkins/jobs/CounterApp/workspace/pom.xml to
com.tinyclouds/CounterWebApp/1.0-SNAPSHOT/CounterWebApp-1.0-SNAPSHOT.pom
[JENKINS] Archiving /root/.jenkins/jobs/CounterApp/workspace/target
/CounterWebApp.war to com.tinyclouds/CounterWebApp/1.0-SNAPSHOT/CounterWebApp-
1.0-SNAPSHOT.war
channel stopped
Deploying /root/.jenkins/jobs/CounterApp/workspace/CounterWebApp.war to
container Tomcat 7.x Remote
  [/root/.jenkins/jobs/CounterApp/workspace/CounterWebApp.war] is not deployed.
Doing a fresh deployment.
  Deploying [/root/.jenkins/jobs/CounterApp/workspace/CounterWebApp.war]
Deploying /root/.jenkins/jobs/CounterApp/workspace/target/CounterWebApp.war to
container Tomcat 7.x Remote
  Redeploying [/root/.jenkins/jobs/CounterApp/workspace/target/CounterWebApp.war]
  Undeploying [/root/.jenkins/jobs/CounterApp/workspace/target/CounterWebApp.war]
  Deploying [/root/.jenkins/jobs/CounterApp/workspace/target/CounterWebApp.war]
Finished: SUCCESS
```

Build execution with test cases

Jenkins allows JUnit-format test results to be published on the dashboard. We need not install any specific plugin for this. If we have test cases already written in JUnit, then it is easy to execute them. Make sure to create a goal or task in the build file for test case execution. In Build Job configuration, click on **Post-build Actions** and select **Publish JUnit test result report**. Provide the location for the **Test report XMLs** files and save the build job configuration.

Execute the build by clicking on **Build Now**. Once the build has finished, click on the **Test Result** link on the dashboard.

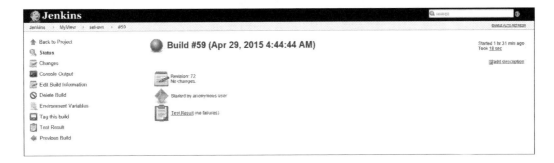

Click on the package link to get detailed test results on the summary page.

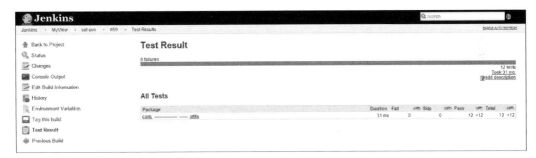

Click on the class link to get detailed test results on the page.

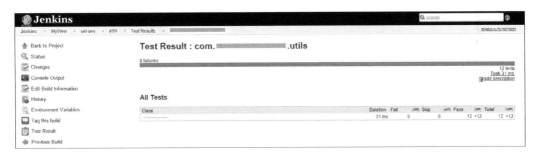

Verify all tests name, the duration, and the status, as shown in the following figure:

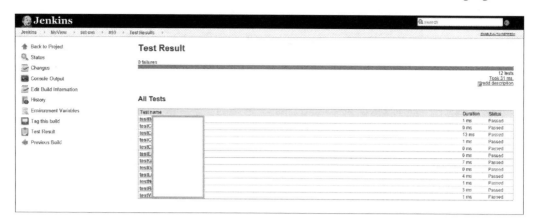

Verify by clicking on the individual link of each test case on the Jenkins dashboard.

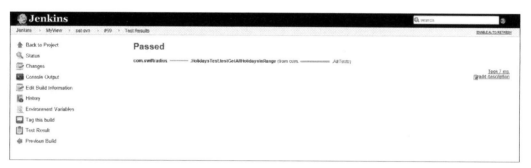

We have already configured the Dashboard View plugin to display the Test Statistics Chart and the Test Trend Chart.

Verify the number of successful, failed or skipped tests, as well as the percentage on the customized view, as shown in the following screenshot.

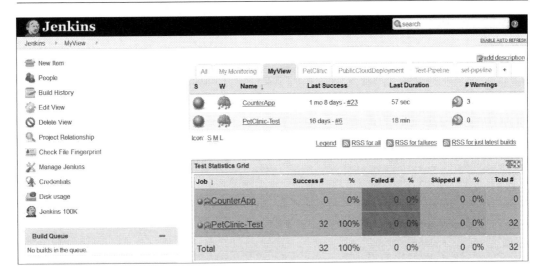

Verify the Test Trend Chart on the Dashboard View.

Self-test questions

Q1. What is the objective of installing the Dashboard View plugin?

1. To have a portal-like view for Jenkins build jobs
2. To run test cases related to Jenkins build jobs
3. To display build results

Q2. Which are the fields available to create credentials for SVN?

1. **Scope, Username, Password, Description**
2. **Scope, Username, Password**
3. **Username, Password, Description**

Q3. What is the meaning of * * * * * in the **Schedule of Build Trigger** section?

1. Poll SCM Every Day
2. Poll SCM Every Hour
3. Poll SCM Every Minute
4. Poll SCM Every Second

Q4. What are the names of build files in Ant and Maven respectively?

1. `pom.xml, build.xml`
2. `build.xml, pom.xml`
3. `pom.xml, root.xml`
4. `ant.xml, maven.xml`

Summary

We are again at the part of the chapter that gives us a sense of achievement. In this chapter, we have covered how to customize the Jenkins dashboard and display test results based on the build job on the dashboard. We have also created our first build job for a sample Java application. We used build tools such as Ant and Maven for executing build and create artifacts. Finally, we have seen how test cases can be executed, and results can be displayed on the Jenkins portal.

In the next chapter, we will deploy the application to application server directly from Jenkins, and we will also cover an introduction to deploying applications on Amazon Web Services.

4
Implementing Automated Deployment

"Simplicity is prerequisite for reliability"

– Edsger Dijkstra

We have covered the concept of continuous integration, and we also know how to implement it using Jenkins. Now is the time to move to the next step in the application deployment pipeline, that is automated deployment. We will first understand the concept of continuous delivery and continuous deployment, before automated deployment into a Tomcat application server.

This chapter will take one step forward in the deployment pipeline by deploying artifacts in a local or remote application server. It will give an insight into the automated deployment and continuous delivery process.

- Overview of continuous delivery and continuous deployment
- Deploying a file from Jenkins to a Tomcat server

An overview of continuous delivery and continuous deployment

Continuous delivery is the extension of Continuous Integration practices. Application artifacts are production-ready in automated fashion but not deployed in production. Continuous deployment is the extension of continuous delivery, where changes in the application are finally deployed in production. Continuous delivery is a must for DevOps practices. Let's understand how to deploy application artifacts using Jenkins in the following sections.

 For more details on continuous delivery and continuous deployment, visit:

`http://continuousdelivery.com/2010/08/continuous-delivery-vs-continuous-deployment/`

`http://martinfowler.com/books/continuousDelivery.html`

Installing Tomcat

Tomcat is an open source web server and servlet container developed by the **Apache Software Foundation (ASF)**. We will use Tomcat to deploy web applications.

1. Go to `https://tomcat.apache.org` and download Tomcat. Extract all the files to a relevant folder in your system.

2. Change the port number in `conf/server.xml` from `8080` to `9999`.

   ```
   <Connector port="9999" protocol="HTTP/1.1"
               connectionTimeout="20000"
               redirectPort="8443" />
   ```

3. Open the terminal or Command Prompt based on your operating system. Go to the `tomcat` directory. Go to the `bin` folder, and run `startup.bat` or `startup.sh`. The following is an example of `startup.bat` on Windows.

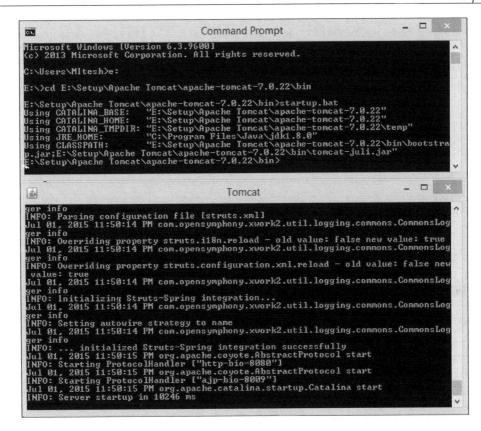

4. Open your browser and visit `http://localhost:9999`. We can also access the Tomcat home page by using the IP address `http://<IP address>:9999`.

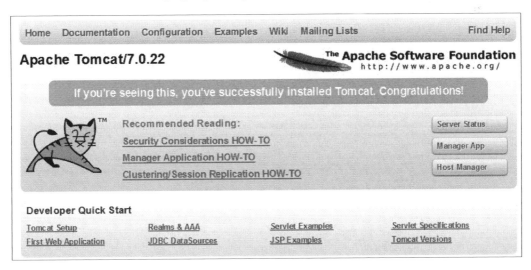

Deploying a war file from Jenkins to Tomcat

We will use the Deploy plugin available at `https://wiki.jenkins-ci.org/x/CAAjAQ` to deploy a `war` file into a specific container.

The Deploy plugin takes the `war/ear` file, and deploys it to a running local or remote application server at the end of a build.

It supports the following containers:

- Tomcat: 4.x/5.x/6.x/7.x
- JBoss: 3.x/4.x
- Glassfish: 2.x/3.x

To deploy a `war` file in a `Websphere` container, use the Deploy WebSphere plugin available at `https://wiki.jenkins-ci.org/x/UgCkAg`.

To deploy a `war` file in a `Weblogic` container, use the WebLogic Deployer plugin available at `https://wiki.jenkins-ci.org/x/q4ahAw`.

1. On the Jenkins dashboard, go to the **Manage Jenkins** link and then click on **Manage Plugins** and install **Deploy plugin**.

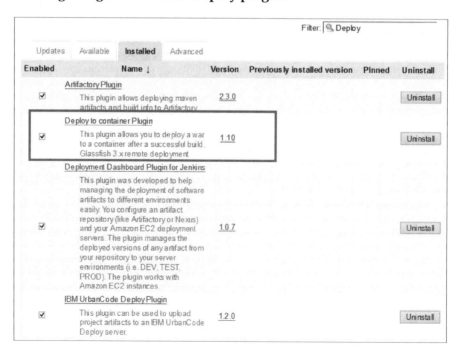

2. Wait until the installation of **Deploy Plugin** is complete.

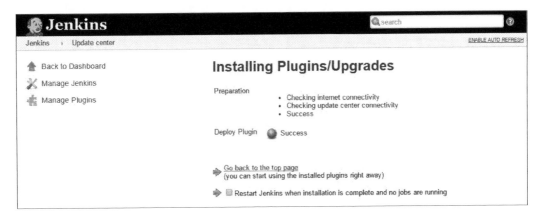

3. Go to the Jenkins dashboard and select any build job. Click on the **Configure** link of the selected build job.

4. Click on the **Add post-build action** button on the configuration page of the relevant job and select **Deploy war/ear to container,** as shown in the following figure.

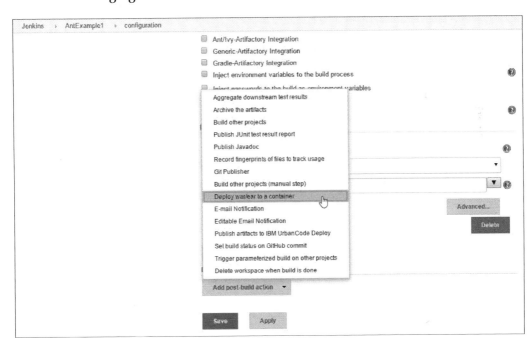

5. It will add **Deploy war/ear to a container** in the **Post-build Actions** section. Provide a **war** file path that is relative to the workspace, and select **Tomcat 7.x** as the container from the available list box, as shown in the following figure.

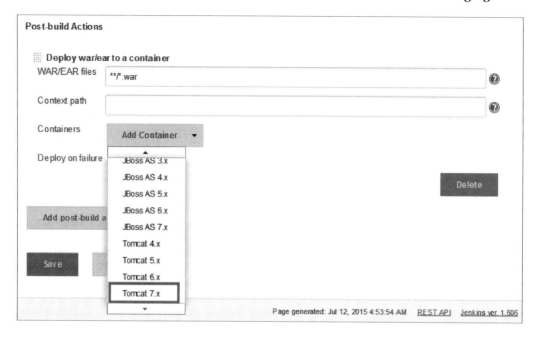

6. Provide **Manager user name** and **Manager password**; in `tomcat-users.xml`, and uncomment the following:

```
<!--
  <role rolename="tomcat"/>
  <role rolename="role1"/>
  <user username="tomcat" password="tomcat" roles="tomcat"/>
  <user username="both" password="tomcat" roles="tomcat,role1"/>
  <user username="role1" password="tomcat" roles="role1"/>
-->
```

7. Add the following in the uncommented section:

```
<role rolename="manager-script"/>
<user username="mitesh51" password="*********" roles="manager-script"/>
```

8. Restart Tomcat, visit `http://localhost:9999/manager/html`, and enter a username and password. Use the same username and password in Jenkins for Manager credentials.

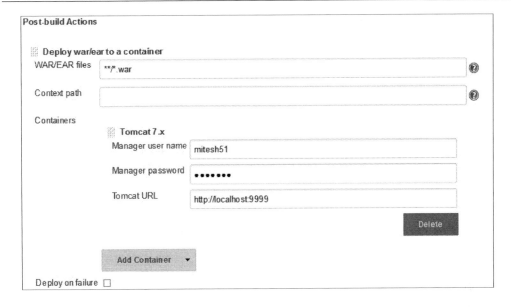

9. Click on **Build Now**.

10. Once the build is complete, verify the console output of the deployment of the application in the Tomcat application server.

```
[workspace] $ /root/.jenkins/tools/hudson.tasks.Ant_AntInstallation/Ant1.9.4/bin/ant
Buildfile: /root/.jenkins/jobs/AntExample1/workspace/build.xml

init:
    [mkdir] Created dir: /root/.jenkins/jobs/AntExample1/workspace/build/classes
    [mkdir] Created dir: /root/.jenkins/jobs/AntExample1/workspace/dist

compile:
    [javac] /root/.jenkins/jobs/AntExample1/workspace/build.xml:16: warning:
'includeantruntime' was not set, defaulting to build.sysclasspath=last; set to false
for repeatable builds
    [javac] Compiling 4 source files to /root/.jenkins/jobs/AntExample1/workspace
/build/classes
    [javac] Note: /root/.jenkins/jobs/AntExample1/workspace/src/com/vaannila
/web/UserController.java uses or overrides a deprecated API.
    [javac] Note: Recompile with -Xlint:deprecation for details.

war:
      [war] Building war: /root/.jenkins/jobs/AntExample1/workspace
/dist/AntExample.war

BUILD SUCCESSFUL
Total time: 13 seconds
Deploying /root/.jenkins/jobs/AntExample1/workspace/dist/AntExample.war to container
Tomcat 7.x Remote
  Redeploying [/root/.jenkins/jobs/AntExample1/workspace/dist/AntExample.war]
  Undeploying [/root/.jenkins/jobs/AntExample1/workspace/dist/AntExample.war]
  Deploying [/root/.jenkins/jobs/AntExample1/workspace/dist/AntExample.war]
Started calculate disk usage of build
Finished Calculation of disk usage of build in 0 seconds
Started calculate disk usage of workspace
Finished Calculation of disk usage of workspace in 0 seconds
Finished: SUCCESS
```

11. Verify the webapps directory in the Tomcat installation directory.

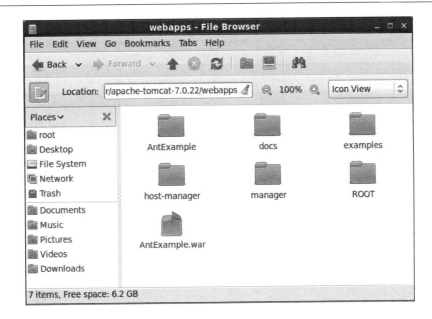

12. Verify the Tomcat manager, and check the status of an application in the Tomcat application server.

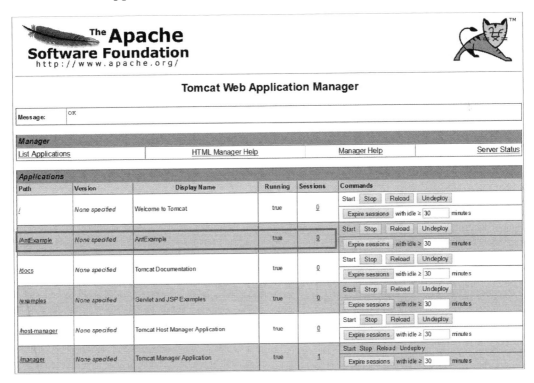

13. If the Tomcat server is installed on a remote server, then use the IP address in the Tomcat URL, as shown in the following figure:

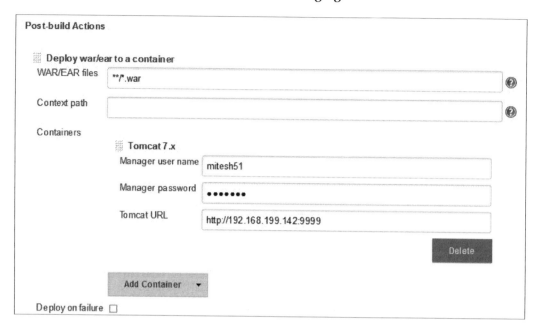

We only need to change the Tomcat URL in case of remote deployment.

Self-test questions

Q1. Continuous delivery and continuous deployment are the same.

1. True
2. False

Q2. How do you enable Tomcat manager access?

1. Start Tomcat
2. Modify `server.xml`
3. Modify `tomcat-users.xml`
4. Modify `web.xml`

Summary

Well done! We are at the end of the chapter; let's summarize what we have covered. We have understood the concept of continuous delivery and continuous deployment. The main concept we have covered here is the deployment of application artifacts in the specific application server after the build is successful.

In the next chapter, we will learn how to manage Jenkins on Cloud, and look at some case studies.

5
Hosted Jenkins

"Productivity is being able to do things that you were never able to do before"

–Franz Kafka

We have understood the concepts of continuous delivery and continuous deployment. We have also seen how to deploy the `war` file from Jenkins to the Tomcat server. Now, we will see how hosted Jenkins can be leveraged. Different service providers offer Jenkins as a service. We will see how OpenShift and CloudBees provide Jenkins to users.

This chapter describes details on how to use hosted Jenkins, which is provided by popular PaaS providers, such as Red Hat OpenShift and CloudBees. This chapter also covers details on how various customers are using Jenkins based on their requirements. This chapter will explore details on how to use Cloud-related plugins in Jenkins for effective usage of Jenkins. We will cover the following topics in this chapter:

- Exploring Jenkins in OpenShift PaaS
- Exploring Jenkins in the Cloud – CloudBees
- An overview of CloudBees Enterprise Plugins
- Jenkins case studies from CloudBees

Exploring Jenkins in OpenShift PaaS

OpenShift Online is a public PaaS—application development and hosting platform from Red Hat. It automates the process of provisioning and deprovisioning, management, and scaling of applications. This supports command-line client tools and a web management console to launch and manage applications easily. The Jenkins app is provided by OpenShift Online. OpenShift Online has a free plan.

1. To sign up for OpenShift Online, visit `https://www.openshift.com/app/account/new`.

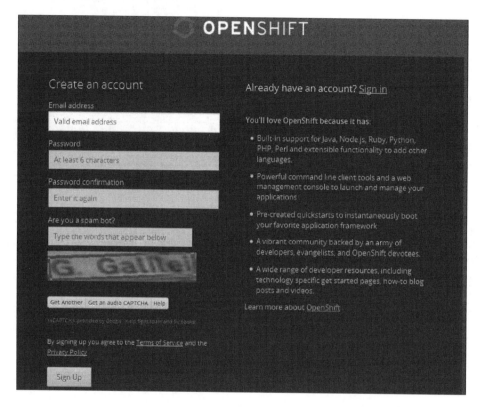

2. Once you sign up, you will get the welcome screen at `https://openshift.redhat.com/app/console/applications`.

3. Click on **Create your first application now**.

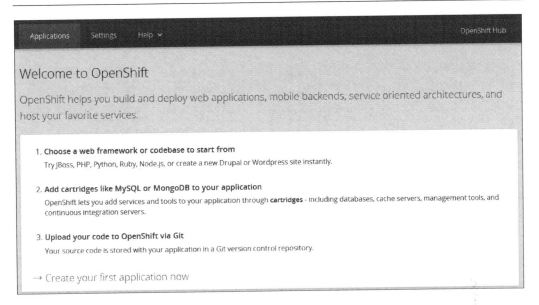

4. Choose a type of application, in our case, select **Jenkins Server**.

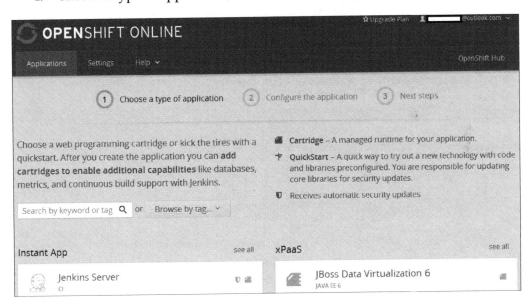

5. Give **Public URL** for your Jenkins server, as shown in the following screenshot:

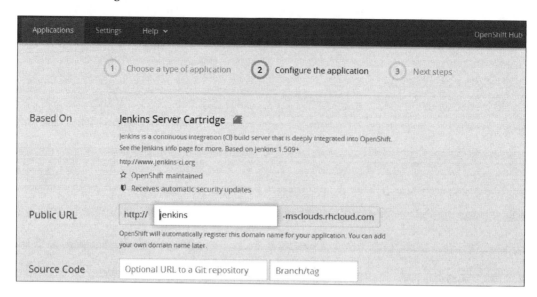

6. Click on **Create Application**.

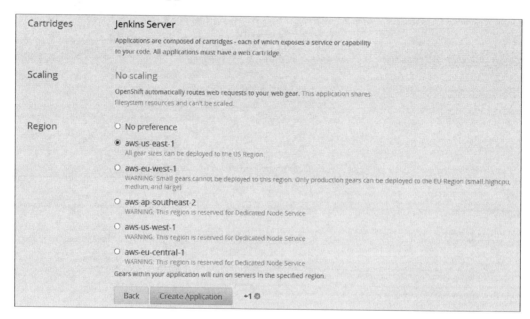

7. Click on **visit app in the browser**.

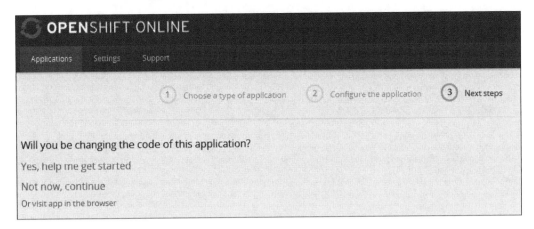

8. Access the Jenkins in the web browser. Then, log in with the provided credentials in the OpenShift dashboard.

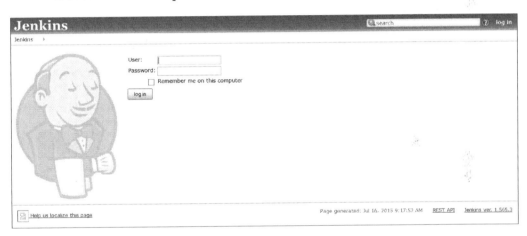

9. The following is the screenshot of the Jenkins dashboard:

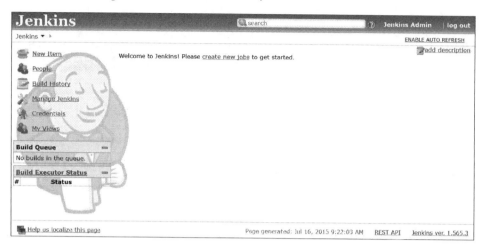

Exploring Jenkins in the Cloud – CloudBees

DEV@cloud is a hosted Jenkins service in a secure, multi-tenanted environment managed by CloudBees. It runs a specific version of Jenkins, along with a selected version of plugins which are well supported with that version. All updates and patches are managed by CloudBees, and limited customization is available.

1. Go to `https://www.cloudbees.com/products/dev` and subscribe.

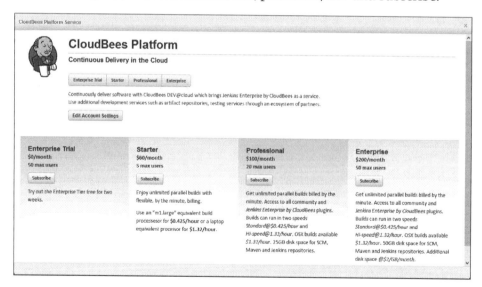

2. Once we complete subscription process, we will get the dashboard of CloudBees, as shown in following screenshot. Click on **Builds**.

3. We will get the Jenkins dashboard, as shown in the following screenshot:

4. Click on **Manage Jenkins** to configure and install plugins.

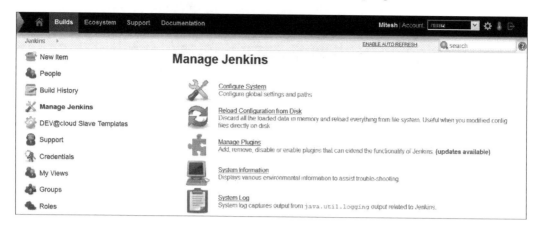

Before configuring a build job, we need to store the source code of an application in the repository service provided by CloudBees. Click on **Ecosystem**, and then click on **Repositories**.

5. Click on the subversion repositories or **Add Repository**, and get the URL of the repository.

6. Click on the application folder to import it into the subversion repository provided by CloudBees. Use TortoiseSVN or any SVN client to import the code.

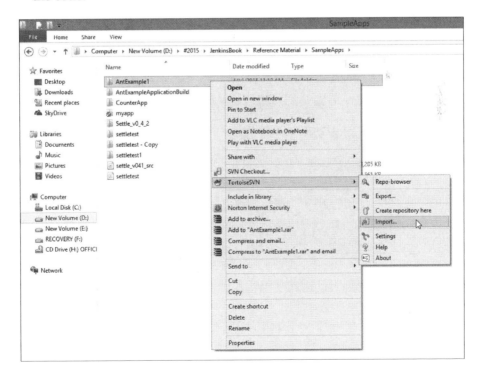

7. Provide the URL of a repository we copied from CloudBees, and click on **OK**.

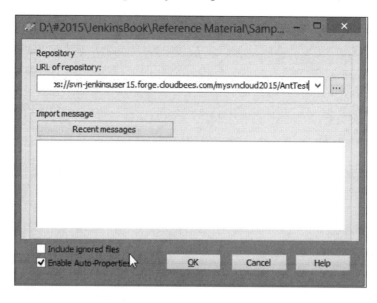

8. Provide authentication information (the username and password are same as our CloudBees account).

   Click on **OK**.

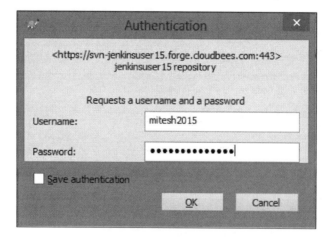

The import process will take some time based on the size of the source files.

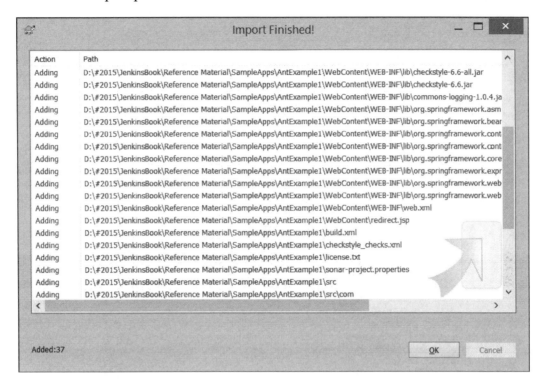

9. Verify the Repository URL on the browser, and we will find the recently imported project in it.

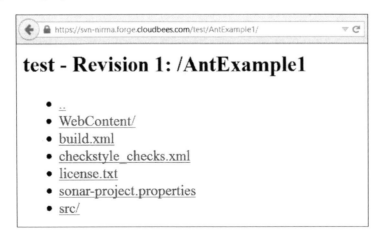

10. Verify the Jenkins dashboard after the successful import operation.

11. Click on **New Item** on the Jenkins dashboard. Select **Freestyle project**, and provide a name for a new build job. Click on **OK**.

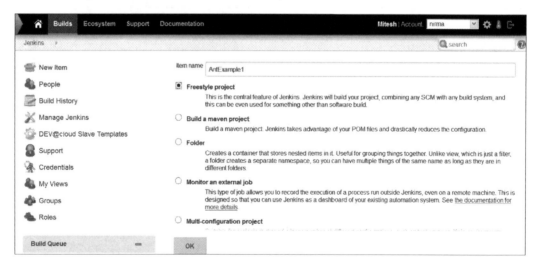

12. The configuration page will allow us to configure various settings specific to the build job.

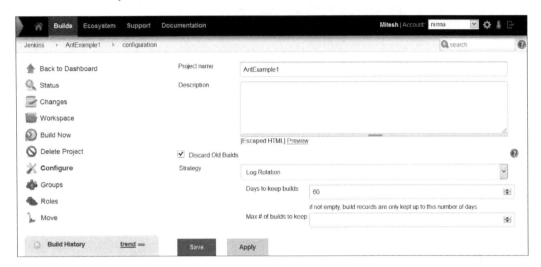

13. Configure the **Subversion** repository in the build job.

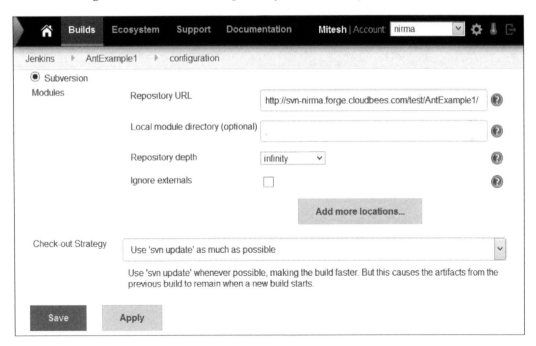

14. Click on **Apply**, and then click on **Save**.

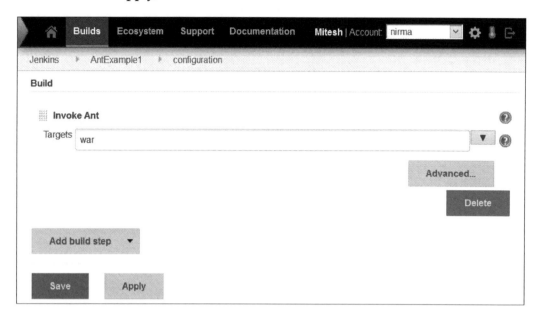

15. Click on **Build Now**.

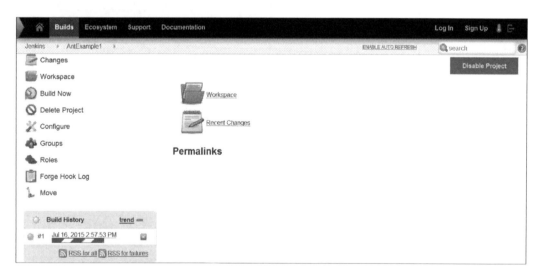

Verify Console Output.

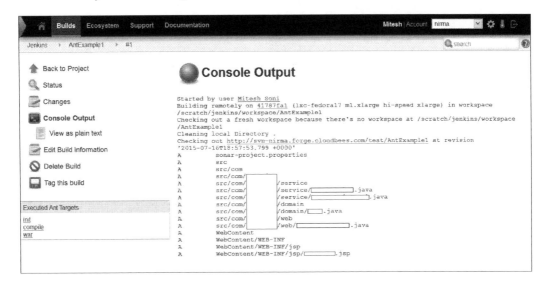

Then, it will compile the source files, and create a `war` file based on the `build.xml` file, as this is an Ant-based project.

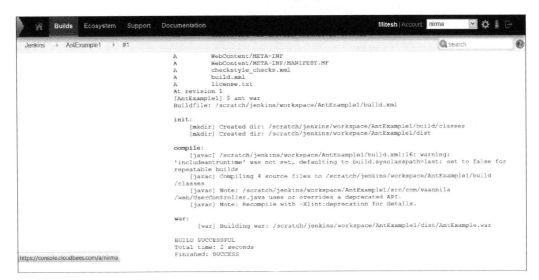

16. Verify the Jenkins dashboard for a successful build.

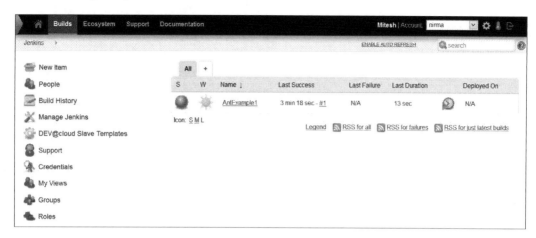

An overview of CloudBees Enterprise Plugins

The following are some important CloudBees Enterprise Plugins:

Workflow Plugin

It is a complex task to manage software delivery pipelines, and developer and operations teams need to manage complex jobs that can take days to complete. The Workflow plugin supports complex pipelines. The plugin uses Groovy DSL for workflows, and it also provides the facility to pause and restart jobs, to and from both master and slave failures.

To read more on this, visit `https://www.cloudbees.com/products/cloudbees-jenkins-platform/team-edition/features/workflow-plugin`.

Checkpoints Plugin

Let's consider a scenario where a long running build job fails almost at its end phase. This can hamper delivery schedules. The Checkpoints plugin provides the facility to restart workflows at checkpoints. Hence, it eliminates delays due to master and slave failures. In addition, it can help to survive Jenkins and infrastructure failures.

To read more on this, visit `https://www.cloudbees.com/products/jenkins-enterprise/plugins/checkpoints-plugin`.

Role-based Access Control Plugin

Authentication and authorization plays a significant role in the security aspect. The authorization strategy can help to control access to Jenkins jobs effectively. It is also essential to set permissions at the project level and visibility. The **Role-based Access Control (RBAC)** plugin provided by CloudBees provides the following features:

- To define various security roles
- To assign rules to groups
- To assign roles globally or at an object level
- To delegate management of groups for specific objects to users

To read more about the Role-based Access Control Plugin, visit `https://www.cloudbees.com/products/jenkins-enterprise/plugins/role-based-access-control-plugin`.

High Availability Plugin

The downtime of Jenkins master caused by software or hardware affects the entire product team. It is vital to bring Jenkins master up in quick time, and this will take many hours. The High Availability plugin eliminates downtime due to master failures, by keeping multiple masters as backups. A backup master automatically boots up when the failure of the master is detected. This plugin makes failure detection and recovery an automatic process and not manual.

To read more on this, visit `https://www.cloudbees.com/products/jenkins-enterprise/plugins/high-availability-plugin`.

VMware ESXi/vSphere Auto-Scaling Plugin

Let's consider a scenario where you need multiple slaves for Jenkins running in your existing infrastructure to utilize underutilized capacity of your virtualized infrastructure based on VMware. The VMware vCenter Auto-Scaling plugin allows you to create slave machines that are available in your VMware-based virtualized infrastructure. It is possible to configure pools of virtual machines that have identical and multiple VMs.

The following actions are allowed on VMs:

- Power on
- Power off/suspend
- Revert to the last snapshot

To read more, visit `https://www.cloudbees.com/products/jenkins-enterprise/plugins/vmware-esxivsphere-auto-scaling-plugin`.

To find details on all plugins provided by CloudBees, visit `https://www.cloudbees.com/products/jenkins-enterprise/plugins`.

Jenkins case studies from CloudBees

We will cover some case studies from CloudBees, where Jenkins is used effectively.

Apache jclouds

Apache jclouds is an open source multi-cloud toolkit that provides the facility to manage workloads on multiple clouds. It was created on the Java platform, and provides complete control to use cloud platform-specific features to create and manage applications. It provides seamless portability across various cloud platforms. Apache jclouds support 30 cloud providers and cloud software stacks such as Joyent, Docker, SoftLayer, Amazon EC2, OpenStack, Rackspace, GoGrid, Azure, and Google. Apache jclouds has a remarkable user base such as CloudBees, Jenkins, Cloudify, cloudsoft, Twitter, Cloudswitch, enStratus, and so on.

Challenge

The jclouds community uses Jenkins CI for continuous integration. Day by day, it was getting more difficult to manage and maintain Jenkins, and it was a costly affair. Managing Jenkins was a time-consuming and tedious task. Most of the time developers were involved in the managing of Jenkins, and not in writing the code to make jclouds more effective.

Solution

The jclouds team explored PaaS offerings available in the market and considered CloudBees, which will help them to eliminate infrastructure management and maintenance. It was recognized by the jclouds team that it is easy to shift the Jenkins CI work to DEV@cloud and immediately gain productivity benefits from developers. Almost 4 hours were saved weekly from the maintenance activity of Jenkins.

Benefits

- 100% focus on software development, by eliminating activities such as server reboots, server sizing, software updates, and patches, as they are automatically performed from within the CloudBees service

- 33% increase in developer productivity

- Technical support from CloudBees for Jenkins CI issues

To read more about this case study, visit `https://www.cloudbees.com/casestudy/jclouds`.

Global Bank

Global Bank is one of the top Global Financial Institutions. It offers corporate and investment banking services, private banking services, credit card services and investment management. It has a substantial international presence.

Challenge

Global Bank's existing process was suffering from a fragmented build process, non-approved software versions, and a lack of technical support. There was a pool of central control or management, and standardization of the process. Build assets were not accessible all the time. There was a need for secure automated process for application build services with audit capabilities. Jenkins provided standardization along with other benefits of a centralized management with robustness and the availability of useful plugins. After using open source Jenkins, the financial institution faced other challenges that were not available in open source Jenkins. More features were needed for approvals, security, backup, and audit.

Solution

To overcome existing challenges, Global Bank evaluated and selected CloudBees Jenkins Enterprise, considering the additional plugins for high availability, backup, security, and job organization, and the ability to obtain technical support for open source Jenkins and open source Jenkins plugins. Global Bank utilized technical support from CloudBees for setting up CloudBees Jenkins Enterprise.

Benefits

- RBAC Plugin provides security and additional enterprise-level functionality. The Folders plugin offers version control and ensures that only approved software versions are shared.

- Half a day of development time is saved per application, by eliminating the need of monitoring the local instance of the build for each application.

- Availability of technical support capabilities.

To read more, visit `https://www.cloudbees.com/casestudy/global-bank`.

Service-Flow

Service-Flow provides online integration services, to connect the disparate IT service management tools used by organizations and various stakeholders. It provides features to create ticket automatically, ticket information exchange, and ticket routing. It has adapters for many ITSM tools such as ServiceNow and BMC, as well as Microsoft Service Manager Fujitsu, Atos, Efecte, and Tieto.

Challenge

Service-Flow wanted to build its own service without using any of the generic integration tools for achieving agility. Service-Flow had several requirements, such as focus on agility, which required a platform for rapid development and frequent incremental updates, support for Jenkins, control over data, reliability, and availability.

Solution

Service-Flow used the CloudBees platform to build and deploy its ITSM integration service. DEV@cloud has been utilized by establishing the version control repository, coding first Java classes, setting up some basic Jenkins jobs, running unit tests, executing integration tests, and other quality checks. The Service-Flow service is in the cloud with a rapidly growing customer base by adding new features using the CloudBees platform.

Benefits

- Development time reduced by 50 percent with production release in three months

- Updates deployed multiple times a week without service downtime

- Availability of 99.999 percent achieved in production

To read more, visit `https://www.cloudbees.com/casestudy/service-flow`.

For more case studies, visit `https://www.cloudbees.com/customers`.

Self-test questions

Q1. What is true about Workflow Plugin provided by CloudBees?

1. To pause and restart jobs, to and from both master and slave failures
2. To manage software delivery pipelines
3. It uses Groovy DSL for workflows
4. All of the above

Q2. What are the features of RBAC Plugin provided by CloudBees?

1. To define various security roles
2. To assign rules to groups
3. To assign role globally or at an object level
4. All of the above

Q3. What actions can be performed by VMware ESXi/vSphere Auto-Scaling Plugin provided by CloudBees?

1. Power on
2. Power off/suspend
3. Revert to the last snapshot
4. All of the above

Summary

The interesting thing about the ending of a chapter is: each chapter that is ending leads you to a new beginning. We know how to configure, manage, and use Jenkins on Cloud service models such as PaaS, RedHat OpenShift, and CloudBees. We also covered some interesting enterprise plugins from CloudBees, which add a lot of flexibility and value. In the last section, we have all provided details on various case studies on how Jenkins proved to be beneficial to a lot of organizations, and how they leveraged functionality of Jenkins to gain a competitive edge.

6
Managing Code Quality and Notifications

"Limit your burden by making very small incremental changes"

–Anonymous

We saw how various customers are using Jenkins on Cloud, based on their requirements. We also saw cloud-based offerings from Red Hat OpenShift and CloudBees, and case studies to understand how Jenkins is used effectively. Now, it is time to know about additional aspects of code quality inspection and notification on build failure.

This chapter will teach you how to integrate static code analysis behavior into Jenkins. Code quality is an extremely vital feature that impacts application's effectiveness and by integrating it with sonar, Checkstyle, FindBugs, and other tools, the user gets an insight into problematic portions of code.

- Integration with Sonar
- Exploring Static code analysis Plugins
- E-mail Notifications on Build status

Integration with Sonar

Quality of code is one of the important facets of DevOps culture. It provides quality checks that highlight the level of reliability, security, efficiency, portability, manageability, and so on. It helps to find bugs or possibility of bugs in the source code and sets culture to align with coding standards in the organization.

SonarQube is the open source platform for continuous inspection of code quality. It supports Java, C#, PHP, Python, C/C++, Flex, Groovy, JavaScript, PL/SQL, COBOL, Objective-C, Android development, and so on. It provides reports on coding standards, code coverage, complex code, unit tests, duplicated code, potential bugs, comments, design and architecture.

1. Go to `http://www.sonarqube.org/downloads/`, and download SonarQube 5.1.

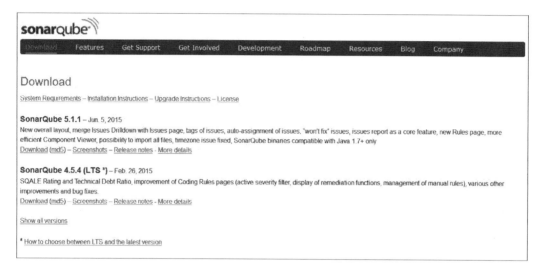

2. Extract files, and it will look similar to the following screenshot:

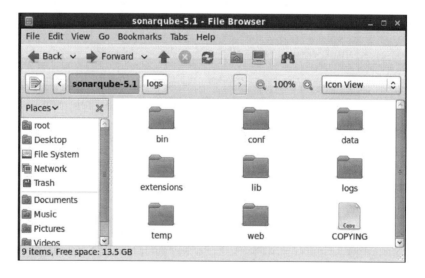

3. Go to the `bin` folder to run SonarQube based on the operating system on which you want to run Sonar.

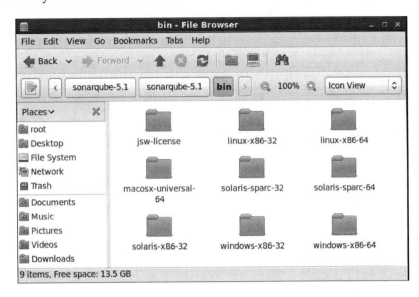

4. Select a folder based on your platform, in our case, we are installing it on CentOS, and so we will select `linux-x86-64`.

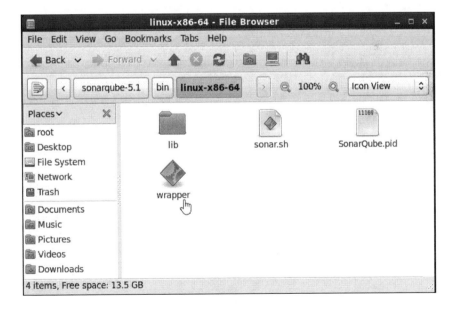

5. Open the terminal and go to the SonarQube home directory; go to `bin/linux-x86-64/` and run `sonar.sh`. We need to use parameters with `sonar.sh`, as shown in the following usage:

```
[root@localhost linux-x86-64]# ./sonar.sh
```

```
Usage: ./sonar.sh { console | start | stop | restart | status | dump }
```

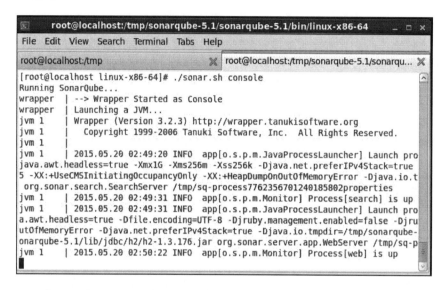

6. Visit `http://localhost:9000/` or `http://<IP address>:9000/`.

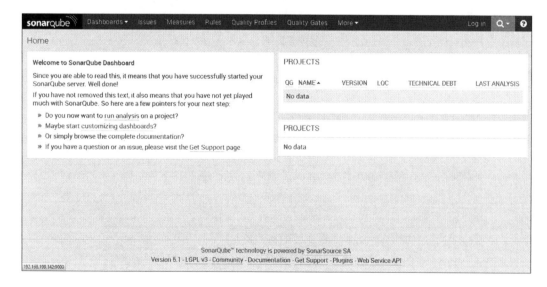

7. Explore **Rules** in the SonaQube dashboard.

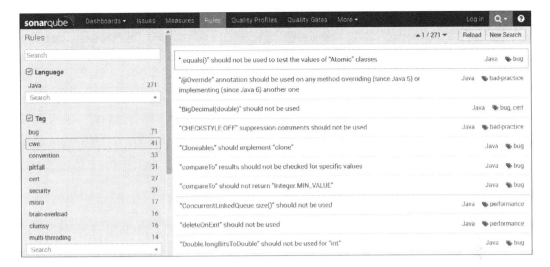

8. Verify **Settings** in the SonaQube dashboard.

9. Create `sonar-project.properties`, and save it in a repository where the project is stored:

```
# must be unique in a given SonarQube instance
sonar.projectKey=Ant:project
# this is the name displayed in the SonarQube UI
sonar.projectName=Ant project
sonar.projectVersion=1.0
sonar.sources=src
```

10. Install the SonarQube plugin in Jenkins. To know more on this, visit
    `https://wiki.jenkins-ci.org/display/JENKINS/SonarQube+plugin`.

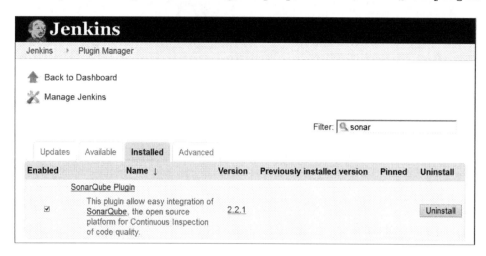

11. Click on **Manage Jenkins** and go to **Configure System**. Go to the **SonarQube**
    section, and configure SonarQube in Jenkins.

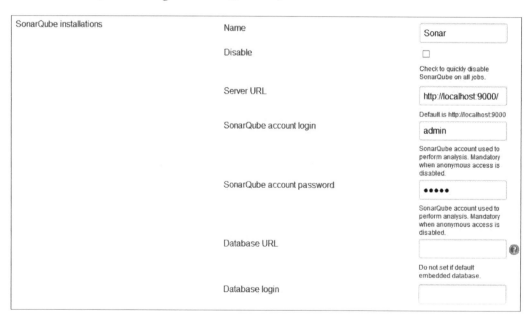

12. Add Build step to **Invoke Standalone SonarQube Analysis** in a build Job.

13. Run the build job, and if you get a certificate error, execute the `svn export` command to solve the certificate issue.

```
ERROR: Error during Sonar runner execution
org.sonar.runner.impl.RunnerException: Unable to execute Sonar
        at
org.sonar.runner.impl.BatchLauncher$1.delegateExecution(BatchLauncher.java:91)
        at org.sonar.runner.impl.BatchLauncher$1.run(BatchLauncher.java:75)
        at java.security.AccessController.doPrivileged(Native Method)
        at org.sonar.runner.impl.BatchLauncher.doExecute(BatchLauncher.java:69)
        at org.sonar.runner.impl.BatchLauncher.execute(BatchLauncher.java:50)
        at org.sonar.runner.api.EmbeddedRunner.doExecute(EmbeddedRunner.java:102)
        at org.sonar.runner.api.Runner.execute(Runner.java:100)
        at org.sonar.runner.Main.executeTask(Main.java:70)
        at org.sonar.runner.Main.execute(Main.java:59)
        at org.sonar.runner.Main.main(Main.java:53)
Caused by: java.lang.IllegalStateException: The svn blame command [svn blame --xml
--non-interactive -x -w src/com/vaannila/domain/User.java] failed: svn: OPTIONS of
'https://192.168.1.12/svn/MS/AntExample1/src/com/vaannila/domain/User.java':
authorization failed: Could not authenticate to server: rejected Basic challenge
(https://192.168.1.12)

        at org.sonar.plugins.scm.svn.SvnBlameCommand.blame(SvnBlameCommand.java:110)
        at
org.sonar.plugins.scm.svn.SvnBlameCommand.access$000(SvnBlameCommand.java:45)
        at org.sonar.plugins.scm.svn.SvnBlameCommand$1.call(SvnBlameCommand.java:91)
        at org.sonar.plugins.scm.svn.SvnBlameCommand$1.call(SvnBlameCommand.java:88)
        at java.util.concurrent.FutureTask.run(FutureTask.java:262)
        at
java.util.concurrent.ThreadPoolExecutor.runWorker(ThreadPoolExecutor.java:1145)
        at
java.util.concurrent.ThreadPoolExecutor$Worker.run(ThreadPoolExecutor.java:615)
        at java.lang.Thread.run(Thread.java:745)
ERROR:
ERROR: Re-run SonarQube Runner using the -X switch to enable full debug logging.
Build step 'Invoke Standalone SonarQube Analysis' marked build as failure
Started calculate disk usage of build
Finished Calculation of disk usage of build in 0 seconds
Started calculate disk usage of workspace
Finished Calculation of disk usage of workspace in 0 seconds
Finished: FAILURE
```

14. Execute the `svn export` command to solve certificate issue on a virtual machine where SonarQube and Jenkins are installed, as shown in the following screenshot:

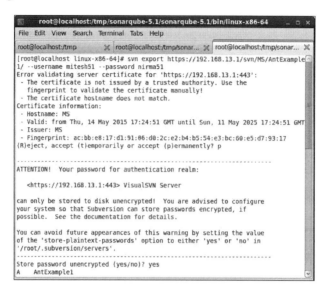

15. Run the build job.

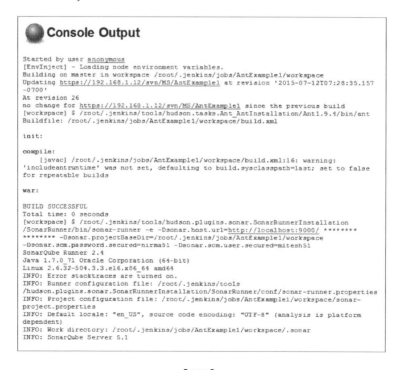

16. Verify the Sonar execution steps in the console.

```
07:28:49.303 INFO  - Cross-project analysis disabled
07:28:49.389 INFO  - Sensor CPD Sensor (done) | time=87ms
07:28:49.390 INFO  - No quality gate is configured.
07:28:49.437 INFO  - Compare to previous analysis (2015-07-12)
07:28:49.444 INFO  - Compare over 30 days (2015-06-12, analysis of Sun Jul 12
07:14:15 PDT 2015)
07:28:50.399 INFO  - Execute decorators...
07:28:51.907 INFO  - Store results in database
07:28:52.608 INFO  - Analysis reports generated in 36ms, dir size=1 KB
07:28:52.622 INFO  - Analysis reports compressed in 14ms, zip size=3 KB
07:28:52.716 INFO  - Analysis reports sent to server in 94ms
07:28:52.716 INFO  - ANALYSIS SUCCESSFUL, you can browse http://localhost:9000
/dashboard/index/Ant:project
07:28:52.716 INFO  - Note that you will be able to access the updated dashboard once
the server has processed the submitted analysis report.
INFO: ------------------------------------------------------------------------
INFO: EXECUTION SUCCESS
INFO: ------------------------------------------------------------------------
Total time: 15.545s
Final Memory: 13M/124M
INFO: ------------------------------------------------------------------------
Deploying /root/.jenkins/jobs/AntExample1/workspace/dist/AntExample.war to container
Tomcat 7.x Remote
  Redeploying [/root/.jenkins/jobs/AntExample1/workspace/dist/AntExample.war]
  Undeploying [/root/.jenkins/jobs/AntExample1/workspace/dist/AntExample.war]
  Deploying [/root/.jenkins/jobs/AntExample1/workspace/dist/AntExample.war]
Started calculate disk usage of build
Finished Calculation of disk usage of build in 0 seconds
Started calculate disk usage of workspace
Finished Calculation of disk usage of workspace in 0 seconds
Finished: SUCCESS
```

17. Refresh the dashboard of SonarQube, and we will be able to see details on the recently executed build in SonarQube, as shown in the following screenshot:

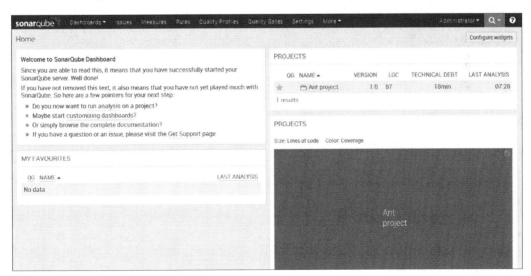

18. To get more details on code verification, click on the project, and we will be able to get details on **Lines of Code**, **Duplications**, **Complexity**, and so on.

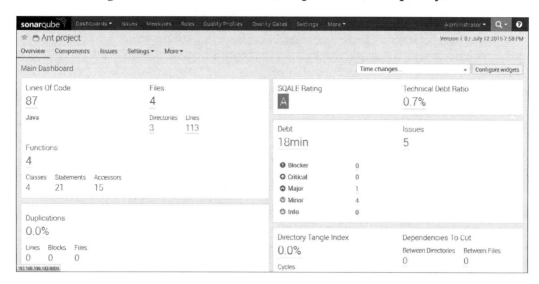

Explore more things on SonarQube and Jenkins integration, as in the following steps.

Exploring Static Code Analysis Plugins

Static Code Analysis Plugins provide utilities for the static code analysis plugins. Jenkins interprets the result files of several static code analysis tools with the use of different plugins for configuration and parsing. We can have more flexibility with these plugins to build exactly what you want.

To install any of these plugins, go to the Jenkins dashboard, click on **Manage Jenkins**, and select the **Manage Plugins** link. Go to the **Available** tab, find the respective plugin, and select it. Click on **Download now**, and install after restart.

All these results are visualized by the same backend. The following plugins use the same visualization:

Checkstyle Plugin

The Checkstyle plugin generates the report for an open source static code analysis program, Checkstyle.

To know more about the Checkstyle plugin, visit https://wiki.jenkins-ci.org/display/JENKINS/Checkstyle+Plugin.

FindBugs Plugin

The FindBugs plugin is supported by the Static Analysis Collector plugin that shows the results in aggregated trend graphs, health reporting, and builds stability.

To learn more about this, visit `https://wiki.jenkins-ci.org/display/JENKINS/FindBugs+Plugin`.

Compiler Warnings Plugin

The Compiler Warnings plugin generates the trend report for compiler warnings in the console log, or in log files.

To know more, visit `https://wiki.jenkins-ci.org/display/JENKINS/Warnings+Plugin`.

To publish the combined results of Checkstyle, FindBugs, and compiler warnings plugins, go to the **Build** section of any job, and click on **Add post-build action** and select **Publish combined analysis results**.

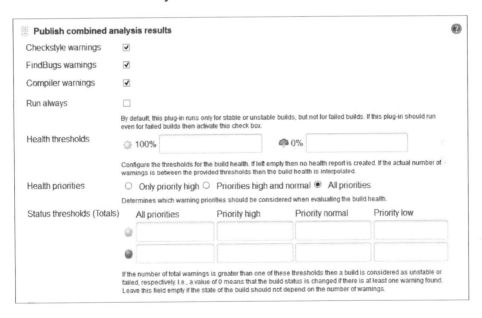

We can also see these results with the use of the Dashboard View plugin.

In the configuration of a Dashboard view, click on **Edit View** and select checkboxes in the **Number of warnings** section. Add **Dashboard Portlets** in different sections for Checkstyle, Compiler, and Findbug.

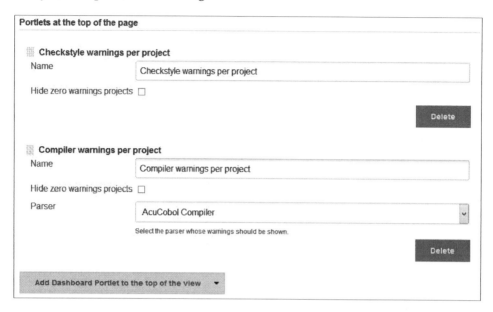

Verify the view after all the changes and running build jobs.

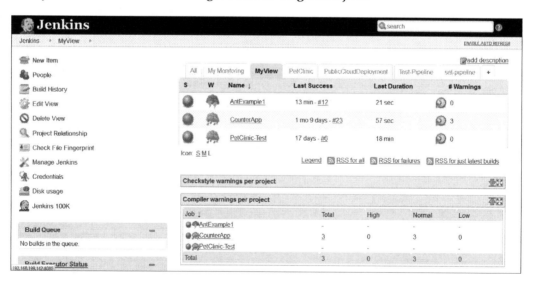

The following plugins are also useful.

DRY Plugin

The DRY plugin shows the duplicate code blocks in your project. It only shows the results of duplicate code checker tools.

To know more, visit `https://wiki.jenkins-ci.org/display/JENKINS/DRY+Plugin`.

PMD Plugin

The PMD plugin scans the `pmd.xml` files in the build workspace, and reports warnings.

To know more, visit `https://wiki.jenkins-ci.org/display/JENKINS/PMD+Plugin`.

Task Scanner Plugin

The Task Scanner plugin scans the workspace files for open tasks and provides a trend report.

To know more, visit `https://wiki.jenkins-ci.org/display/JENKINS/Task+Scanner+Plugin`.

CCM Plugin

The CCM plugin provides details on cyclomatic complexity for .NET code.

To know more, visit `https://wiki.jenkins-ci.org/display/JENKINS/CCM+Plugin`.

Android Lint Plugin

The Android Lint plugin parses the output from the Android lint tool.

To know more, visit `https://wiki.jenkins-ci.org/display/JENKINS/Android+Lint+Plugin`.

OWASP Dependency-Check Plugin

The Dependency-Check Jenkins Plugin features the ability to perform a dependency analysis build.

To know more, visit `https://wiki.jenkins-ci.org/display/JENKINS/`
`OWASP+Dependency-Check+Plugin`.

E-mail notifications on build status

To send an e-mail notification based on build status, we need to configure SMTP details. Click on **Manage Jenkins**, and go to **Configure System**. Go to the **E-mail Notification** section.

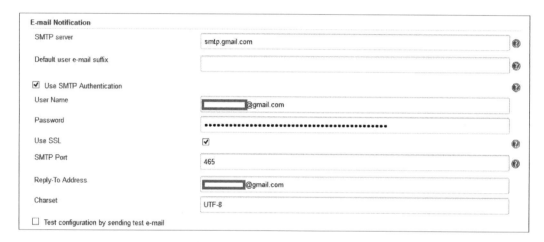

Go to build Job configuration, and click on **Add post-build action**. Select **E-mail Notification**. Provide the recipients list and save.

Run the build job, and a broken build will result in an e-mail notification in the mailbox.

Self-test questions

Q1. Which languages are supported by SonarQube?

1. Java
2. C#
3. PHP
4. Python
5. C/C++
6. JavaScript
7. All of the above

Q2. Which among these is not a Static Code Analysis plugin?

1. DRY Plugin
2. PMD Plugin
3. Task Scanner Plugin
4. FindBugs Plugin
5. None of the above

Summary

Here again, we are at the end of another chapter. We need to remember that every new beginning comes from some other beginning's end. To summarize, we learned how to manage code quality of applications configured, and how to use notification features to send information to developers based on the failed build. We also covered some static code analysis plugins in short, to get some idea about it. In the next chapter, we will learn how to manage and monitor Jenkins.

7
Managing and Monitoring Jenkins

"Fall in the beginning + Fall often + Learn to recover quickly = Faster time to market"

– Anonymous

We learned Sonar integration with Jenkins, an overview of static code analysis plugins, and notification of build status in the last chapter. Now, it's time to focus on management and monitoring of Jenkins.

This chapter gives insight into management of Jenkins nodes and monitoring of them with Java Melody to provide details on utilization of resources. It also covers how to manage and monitor build jobs. This chapter describes basic security configuration in detail that is available in Jenkins for a better access control and authorization. The following is the list of topics that we will cover in this chapter:

- Managing Jenkins master and slave nodes
- Jenkins monitoring with JavaMelody
- Managing disk usage
- Build job-specific monitoring with the Build Monitor plugin
- Managing access control and authorization
- Maintaining role and project-based security
- Managing an admin account
- Audit Trail Plugin—an overview and usage

Managing Jenkins master and slave nodes

A master represents basic installation of Jenkins and handles all tasks for the build system. It can satisfy all user requests and has the capacity to build projects on its own. A slave is a system that is set up to reduce the burden of build projects from the master but delegation behavior depends on the configuration of each project. Delegation can be configured specifically to build job.

1. On the Jenkins dashboard, go to **Manage Jenkins**. Click on **Manage Nodes** link. It will provide information on all nodes, as shown in the following screenshot:

2. To create a slave node, click on **New Node**.

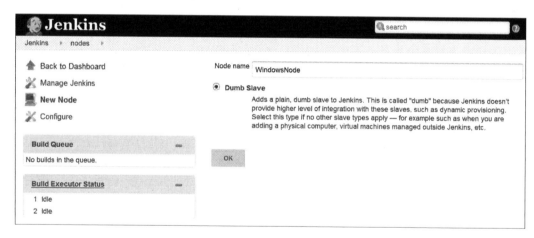

3. Provide **Name, Description, Labels** and so on. Select **Launch slave agents via Java Web Start** as **Launch method**. Provide **Labels**; in our case, it is `java8`:

4. Click on **Save**. It will open a page that gives details on how to launch the slave node.

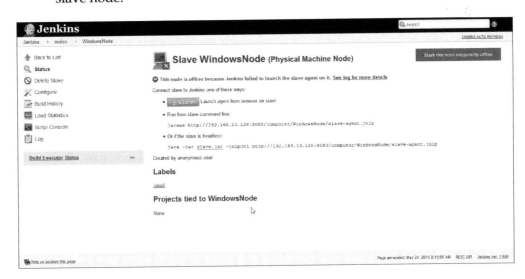

5. Open terminal on the Windows machine and run `javaws` `http://192.168.13.128:8080/computer/WindowsNode/slave-agent.jnlp`.

It will open a dialogue box for downloading the application.

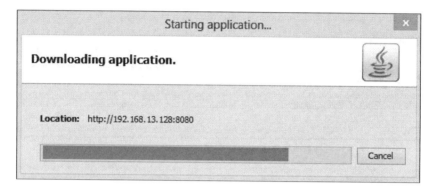

6. Run **Jenkins Remoting Agent**.

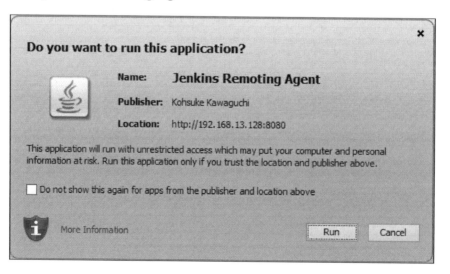

A small window for the Jenkins slave agent will open.

The **slave WindowsNode** will be connected via the JNLP agent.

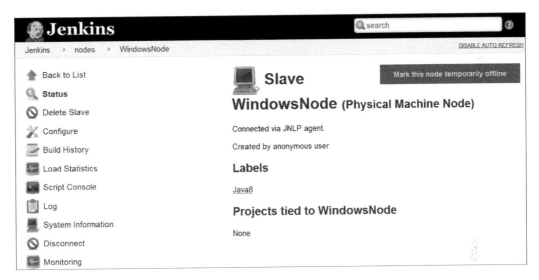

7. On the Jenkins dashboard, go to **Manage Jenkins**. Click on the **Manage Nodes** link. It will provide information on all nodes, as shown in the following screenshot. Verify both the nodes in the **Build Executor Status** section of the leftmost sidebar.

S	Name ↓	Architecture	Clock Difference	Free Disk Space	Free Swap Space	Free Temp Space	Response Time	
	master	Linux (amd64)	In sync	5.86 GB	1.94 GB	5.86 GB	0ms	
	WindowsNode	Windows 8 (amd64)	In sync	215.13 GB	4.27 GB	215.13 GB	3340ms	
	Data obtained	42 sec	42 sec	42 sec	42 sec	42 sec	42 sec	

Refresh status

8. If we want to run a selective build job on to a specific node, then we can configure it build job-wise, as shown in the following screenshot. Check **Restrict where this project can be run** and provide **Label Expression** given to the specific node on the job configuration page.

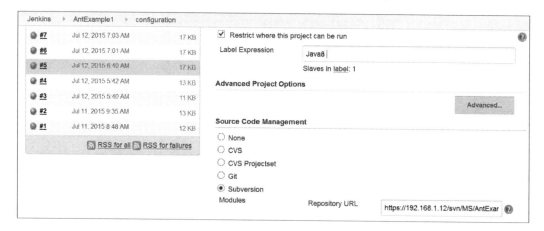

9. Click on **Build Now** to execute build. Verify the console and find building remotely on WindowsNode we configured in the preceding section.

   It will check out the code on slave and perform operations on the specific node only.

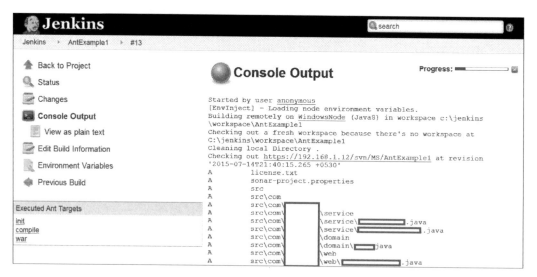

Such configuration is useful where we want to run build job in a specific set of runtime environment, which is available on the specific node.

Jenkins monitoring with JavaMelody

The Monitoring plugin provides monitoring of Jenkins with JavaMelody.
It provides charts of a CPU, memory, system load average, HTTP response time, and so on. It also provides details of HTTP sessions, errors and logs, actions for GC, heap dump, invalidate session(s), and so on. Install the Monitoring plugin from the Jenkins Dashboard.

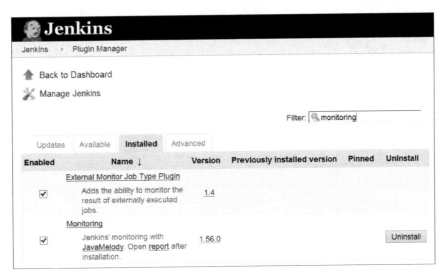

1. On the Jenkins dashboard, click on **Manage Jenkins**. Click on **Monitoring of Jenkins master**, as shown in the following screenshot:

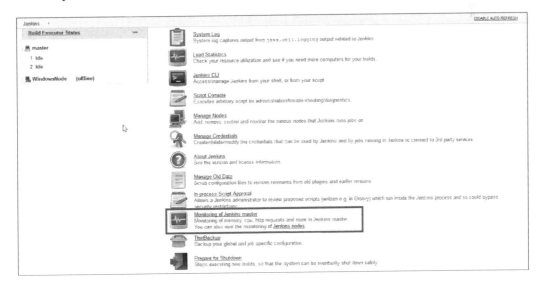

2. It will open the statistics of JavaMelody monitoring, as shown in the following screenshot. Observe all statistics:

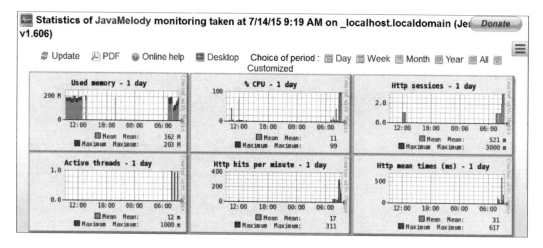

3. Scroll down the page and we will find **Statistics system errors logs**.

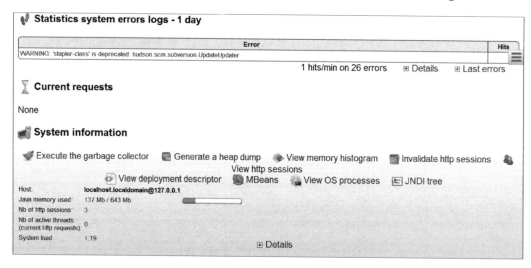

4. To get more information, click on the **Details** link of any section. Statistics of HTTP are as shown in the following figure:

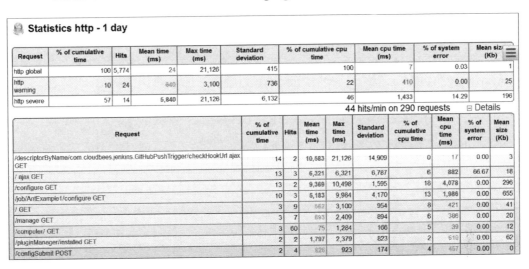

Statistics http - 1 day

Request	% of cumulative time	Hits	Mean time (ms)	Max time (ms)	Standard deviation	% of cumulative cpu time	Mean cpu time (ms)	% of system error	Mean size (Kb)
http global	100	5,774	24	21,126	415	100	7	0.03	1
http warning	10	24	840	3,100	736	22	410	0.00	25
http severe	57	14	5,840	21,126	6,132	46	1,433	14.29	196

44 hits/min on 290 requests   ⊟ Details

Request	% of cumulative time	Hits	Mean time (ms)	Max time (ms)	Standard deviation	% of cumulative cpu time	Mean cpu time (ms)	% of system error	Mean size (Kb)
/descriptorByName/com.cloudbees.jenkins.GitHubPushTrigger/checkHookUrl ajax GET	14	2	10,583	21,126	14,909	0	17	0.00	3
/ ajax GET	13	3	6,321	6,321	6,787	6	882	66.67	18
/configure GET	13	2	9,369	10,498	1,595	18	4,078	0.00	296
/job/AntExample1/configure GET	10	3	5,183	9,984	4,170	13	1,986	0.00	655
/ GET	3	9	562	3,100	954	8	421	0.00	41
/manage GET	3	7	693	2,409	894	6	386	0.00	20
/computer/ GET	3	60	75	1,284	166	5	39	0.00	12
/pluginManager/installed GET	2	2	1,797	2,379	823	2	619	0.00	62
/configSubmit POST	2	4	826	923	174	4	457	0.00	0

5. Explore more at `https://wiki.jenkins-ci.org/display/JENKINS/ Monitoring` to get more details on the Monitoring plugin.

Managing disk usage

1. Disk Usage Plugin records disk usage. Install **Disk Usage Plugin** from the Jenkins dashboard.

2. Once the plugin is successfully installed, we will get the **Disk usage** link on the Manage Jenkins page, as shown in the following screenshot:

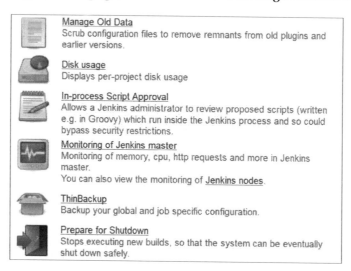

3. The Disk Usage plugin will show project-wise details for all jobs and all workspace. It will also display **Disk Usage Trend**.

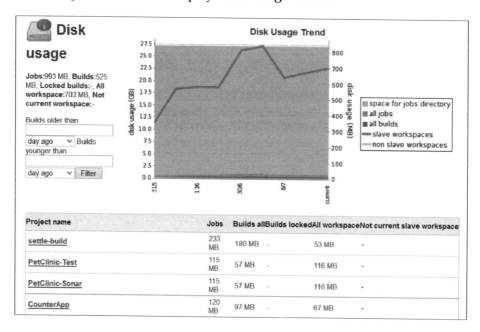

Project name	Jobs	Builds all	Builds locked	All workspace	Not current	slave workspace
settle-build	233 MB	180 MB	-	53 MB	-	
PetClinic-Test	115 MB	57 MB	-	116 MB	-	
PetClinic-Sonar	115 MB	57 MB	-	116 MB	-	
CounterApp	120 MB	97 MB	-	67 MB	-	

To get more details on Disk usage plugin, visit `https://wiki.jenkins-ci.org/display/JENKINS/Disk+Usage+Plugin`.

Build monitoring with Build Monitor Plugin

Build Monitor Plugin provides a detailed view of the status of selected Jenkins jobs. It provides the status and progress of selected jobs and names of people who might be responsible for "breaking the build". This plugin supports the Claim plugin, View Job Filters, Build Failure Analyzer, and CloudBees Folders plugin.

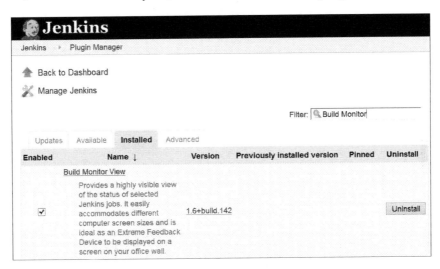

1. The Dashboard View plugin will be used for creating a view that provides details on build job-specific monitoring. Create a new view and select **Build Monitor View**.

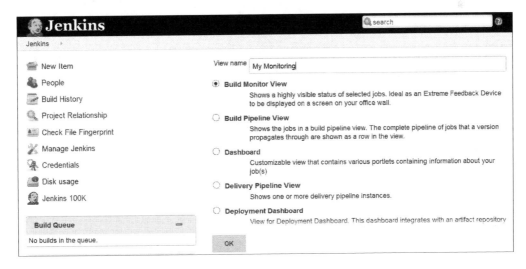

2. Select **Jobs** and save the details.

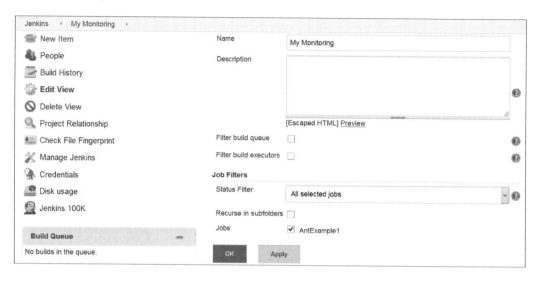

3. Click on the newly created view, and we will get a similar type of screen as given in the following screenshot:

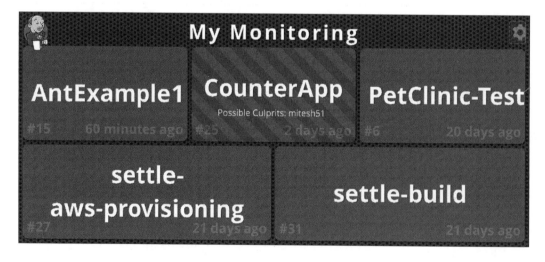

To get more details on plugin, visit `https://wiki.jenkins-ci.org/display/JENKINS/Build+Monitor+Plugin`.

Managing access control and authorization

Jenkins supports several security models, and can integrate with different user repositories.

1. Go to the Jenkins dashboard, click on **Manage Jenkins**, and click on **Configure Global Security**.

2. Click on **Enable security**.

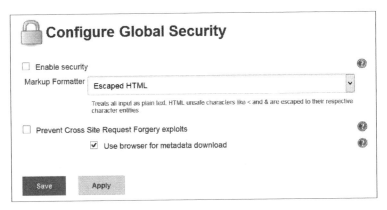

All options will be visible once we enable security, as shown in the following screenshot:

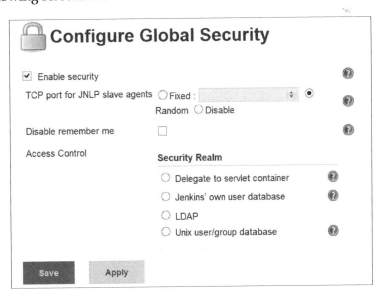

3. Click on **Jenkins' own user database**. Click on **Save**.

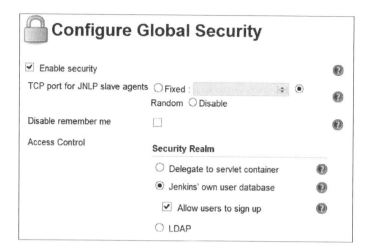

4. Now, click on the **sign up** link on the top-right corner. Provide **Username**, **Password**, **Full name**, and **E-mail address**.

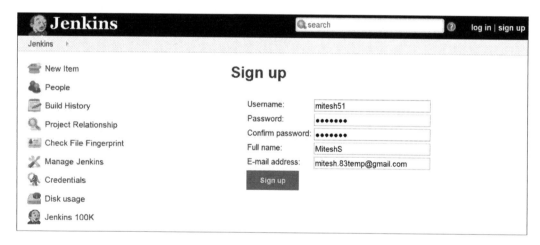

5. Click on the **log in** link on the dashboard.

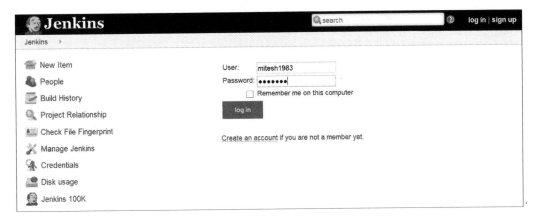

We will get the Jenkins dashboard with the username in the top-right corner.

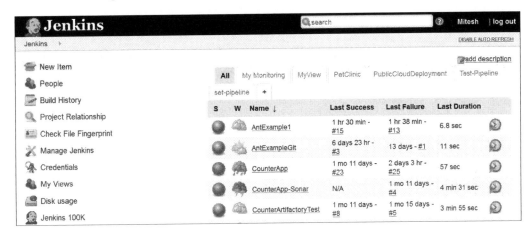

6. Click on **People** to verify all users.

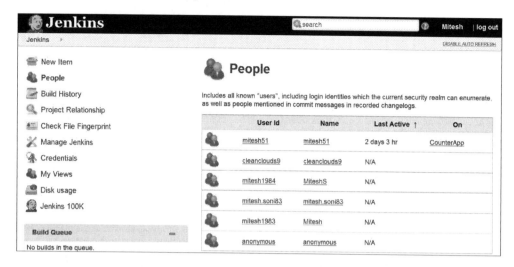

7. On the Jenkins dashboard, click on **Manage Jenkins**. Click on **Manage Users**.

We can edit user details on the same page. This is a subset of users, which also contains auto-created users.

Maintaining roles and project-based security

For authorization, we can define **Matrix-based security** on the **Configure Global Security** page.

1. Add group or user and configure security based on different sections such as **Credentials**, **Slave**, **Job**, and so on.

2. Click on **Save**.

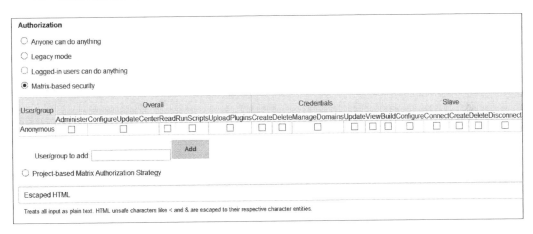

We can use multiple users for matrix-based security, as shown in the following screenshot:

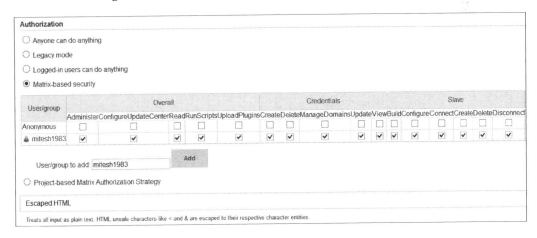

3. Try to access the Jenkins dashboard with a newly added user who has no rights, and we will find the authorization error.

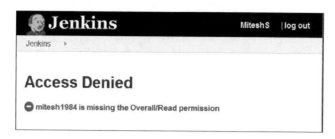

4. Now provide overall read rights; build, read, and workspace rights for job for newly added users.

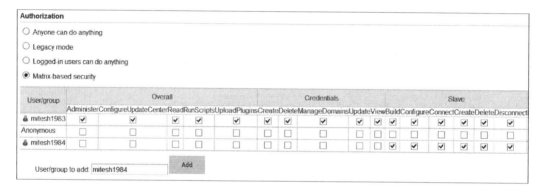

5. Log in with the newly added user and verify that we can see the dashboard. We can't see the **Manage Jenkins** link as we have provided those rights.

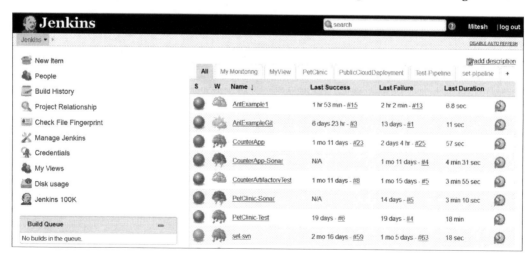

6. Click on any build job. The build link is available as we have given rights but the configure link is not available as rights were not given for it.

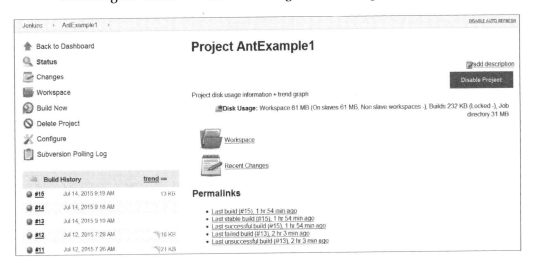

7. We can also set **Project-based Matrix Authorization Strategy**.

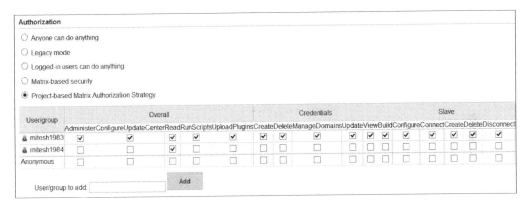

8. Go to a specific build jobs' configuration and **Enable project-based security**.

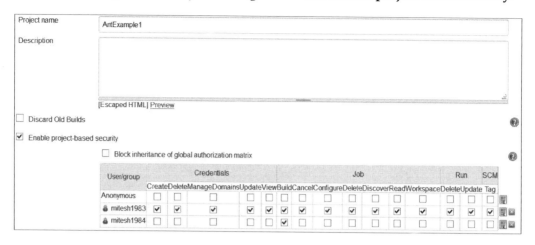

9. Assign rights to different users and log in with the specific username to verify whether authorization strategy is working or not.

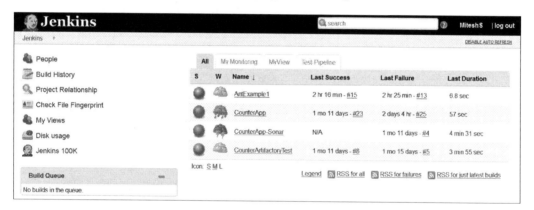

10. Verify the build details also, as shown in the following screenshot:

We've covered basics of security configuration in Jenkins. Explore more on the other options as an exercise. In case, authorization is not correctly set, then it can be corrected by editing `config.xml`. Consider it as self-study.

Audit Trail Plugin – an overview and usage

Audit Trail Plugin keeps a log of users who performed particular Jenkins operations, such as configuring jobs. This plugin adds an **Audit Trail** section in the main Jenkins configuration page.

Install the **Audit Trail Plugin**.

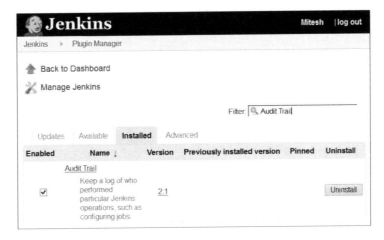

In Jenkins configuration, configure **Loggers**, as shown in the following screenshot:

Stop the Jenkins server and start it again. Run any build job and open log files to verify log records.

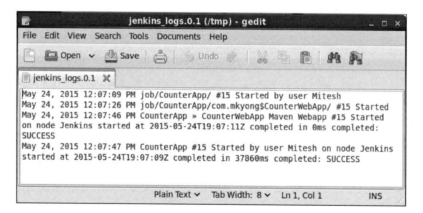

To get more details, visit `https://wiki.jenkins-ci.org/display/JENKINS/ Audit+Trail+Plugin`.

Self-test questions

Q1. What are the different ways to make slave node online?

1. Launch an agent from the browser on slave
2. Run the `slave-agent.jnlp` command from the command line
3. Run `java -jar slave.jar`
4. All of the above

Q2. For what options does Jenkins monitoring provide charts?

1. CPU
2. Memory
3. System load average
4. HTTP response time
5. All of the above

Q3. What are the options for Security Realm in Jenkins?

1. Delegate to Servlet Container
2. Jenkins' own user database
3. LDAP
4. Unix user/group database
5. All of the above

Summary

Whatever good things we build end up building us. In this chapter, we covered concepts of master and slave nodes, how to monitor build jobs, and reporting of statistics with management features. We also understood how to secure Jenkins environment with authentication and authorization configurations by using role-based security. We saw how the audit trail plugin stores audit details in Jenkins.

In the next chapter, we will cover some important plugins that add a significant value to Jenkins. Let's enjoy the last journey before we say goodbye.

8

Beyond Basics of Jenkins – Leveraging "Must-have" Plugins

"Strength and growth come only through continuous effort and struggle."

- Napoleon Hill

In the last chapter, we covered management and monitoring along with security aspects in Jenkins. In security, we understood how authentication and authorization works. Now, it is time to recognize the value added by some important plugins.

This chapter covers advanced usage of Jenkins, which is extremely useful in specific scenarios. Scenario-based usage of specific plugins that help development and operations teams are covered here for better utilization of Jenkins. Some of these plugins are extremely useful in the case of notifications scenario. The following are the main topics that we will cover in this chapter:

- Extended E-mail Plugin
- Workspace cleanup Plugin
- Pre-scm-buildstep Plugin
- Conditional BuildStep Plugin
- EnvInject Plugin
- Build Pipeline Plugin

Extended Email Plugin

Email-ext plugin extends functionality of e-mail notifications provided by Jenkins. It gives more customization in terms of conditions that cause mail notifications and content generation.

You can install this plugin from the Jenkin's dashboard.

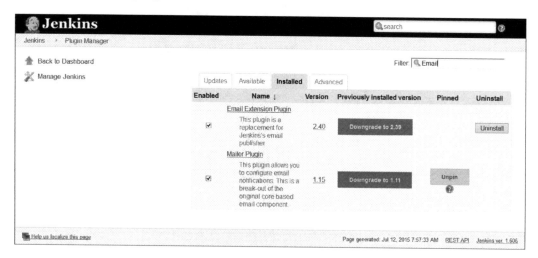

Customization is available in three areas:

- Triggers: We can select the conditions that cause an e-mail notification to be sent
- Content: We can specify the content of each triggered email's subject and body; we can use default environment variables within content
- Recipients: We can specify who should receive an e-mail when it is triggered

In the Jenkins dashboard, click on **Manage Jenkins** and then click on **Configure System**. Go to the **Extended E-mail Notification** section and configure global email-ext properties that should match the settings for your SMTP mail server.

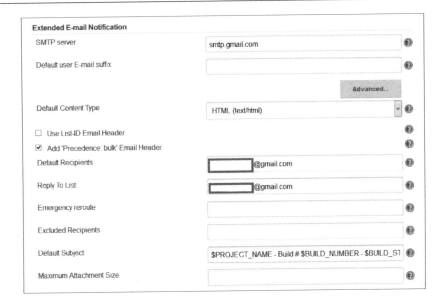

We can also customize the subject, maximum attachment size, default content, and so on.

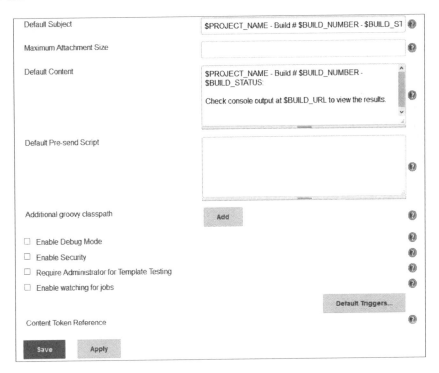

To configure Email-ext specific to build job, enable it in the project configuration page. Select the checkbox labeled **Editable Email Notification** in the **Post-build Actions**. Configure the comma- (or whitespace-) separated list of global recipients, subject, and content. In advanced configuration, we can configure pre-send script, triggers, email tokens, and so on.

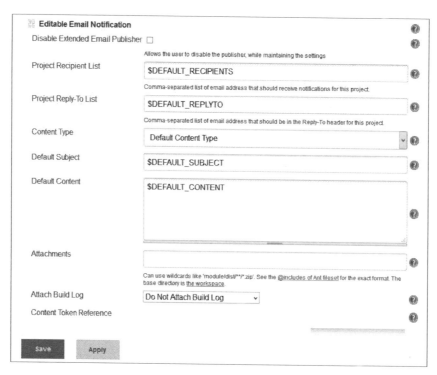

The pre-send script feature allows us to write a script that can modify the `MimeMessage` object prior to sending the message. Triggers allow us to configure conditions that must be met to send an e-mail. The Email-ext plugin uses tokens to allow dynamic data to be inserted into the recipient list, e-mail subject line, or the body. For more details, visit `https://wiki.jenkins-ci.org/display/JENKINS/Email-ext+plugin`.

Workspace cleanup Plugin

The Workspace Cleanup plugin is used to delete the workspace from Jenkins before the build or when a build is finished and artifacts are saved. If we want to start a Jenkins build with a clean workspace or we want to clean a particular directory before each build, then we can effectively use this plugin. Different options are available for deleting the workspace.

You can install this plugin from the Jenkins dashboard.

We can apply patterns for files to be deleted based on the status of the build job. We can add post-build action for workspace deletion.

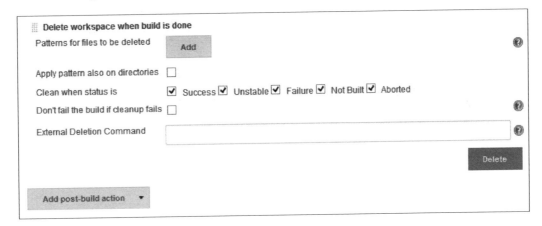

For more details, visit https://wiki.jenkins-ci.org/display/JENKINS/ Workspace+Cleanup+Plugin.

Pre-scm-buildstep Plugin

The Pre-scm-buildstep plugin allows a specific build step to run before SCM checkouts in case we need to perform any build step action on the workspace considering any special requirements such as adding a file with some settings for the SCM, executing some command to create some file, cleanup, or call other scripts that need to be run before checking out.

You can install this plugin from the Jenkins dashboard.

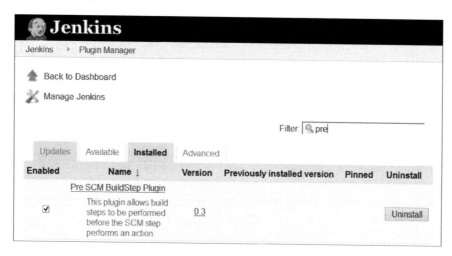

Select conditional steps from the list, as shown in the following screenshot:

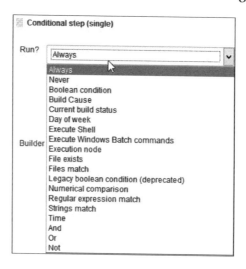

Select the conditional steps based on requirement and provide a list of commands based on operating systems, as shown in the following screenshot:

For more details, visit `https://wiki.jenkins-ci.org/display/JENKINS/pre-scm-buildstep`.

Conditional BuildStep Plugin

The Buildstep plugin allows us to wrap any number of other build steps, controlling their execution based on a defined condition.

You can install this plugin from the Jenkins' dashboard.

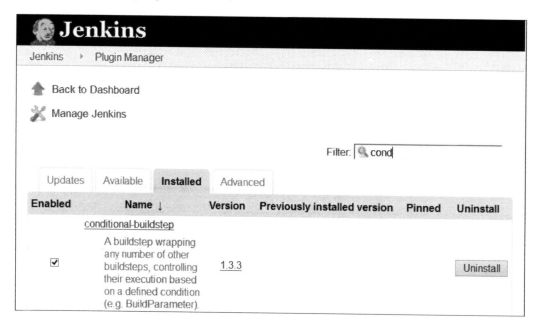

This plugin defines a few core run conditions such as:

- Always/Never: To disable a build step from the job configuration
- Boolean condition: To execute the step if a token expands to a representation of true
- Current status: To execute the build step if the current build status is within the configured/specific range
- File exists/Files match: To execute the step if a file exists, or matches a pattern
- Strings match: To execute the step if the two strings are same
- Numerical comparison: To execute the build step depending on the result of comparing two numbers
- Regular expression match: This provides a regular expression and a label, to execute the build step if the expression matches the label

- **Time/Day of week:** To execute the build job during a specified period of the day or day of the week
- **And/Or/Not:** Logical operations to enable the combining and sense inversion of run conditions
- **Build cause:** To execute the build step depending on the cause of the build, for example, triggered by timer, user, scm-change, and so on
- **Script condition:** Utilize shell script to decide whether a step should be skipped
- **Windows Batch condition:** Utilize windows batch to decide whether a step should be skipped

Select the **Conditional step (single)** from the **Add build step**.

Select the **Conditional steps (multiple)** from the **Add build step**. We can add multiple steps to condition in this conditional step.

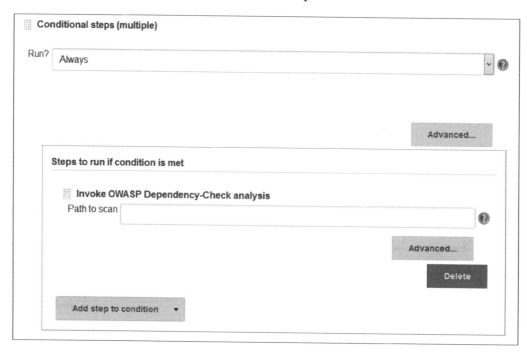

For more details, visit https://wiki.jenkins-ci.org/display/JENKINS/
Conditional+BuildStep+Plugin.

EnvInject Plugin

We know that different environments such as Dev, Test, and Production requires different configuration.

Install this plugin from the Jenkins dashboard.

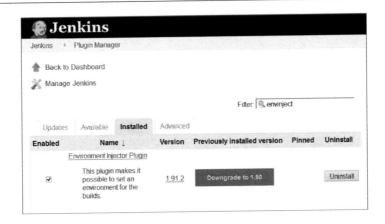

The EnvInject plugin provides the facility to have an isolated environment for different build jobs. The EnvInject plugin injects environment variables at node startup, before or after a SCM checkout for a run, as a build step for a run, and so on. Select **Inject environment variables to the build process** specific to the build job.

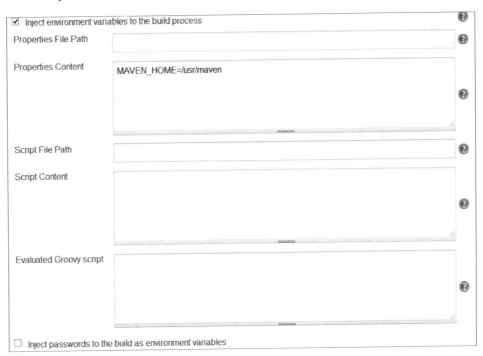

For more details, visit `https://wiki.jenkins-ci.org/display/JENKINS/EnvInject+Plugin`.

Build Pipeline Plugin

Continuous Integration has become a popular practice for application development. The Build Pipeline plugin provides a pipeline view of upstream and downstream connected jobs that typically form a build pipeline with the ability to define manual triggers or approval process. We can create a chain of jobs by orchestrating version promotion through different quality gates before we deploy it in production.

Install this plugin from the Jenkins dashboard.

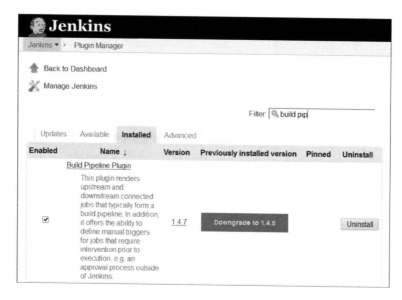

We have already installed the Dashboard View plugin. We will create a pipeline for four build jobs. Let's assume we have four build jobs, as shown in the following diagram, where the objective of each build job is mentioned:

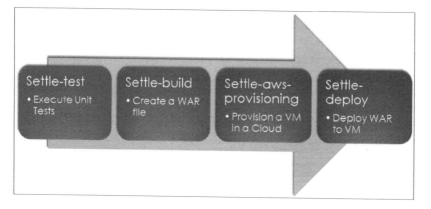

1. Create a new view and select **Build Pipeline View**.

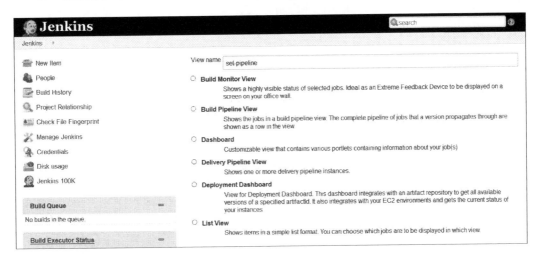

2. Provide a description and select the layout from the configuration on the build pipeline.

3. Select an initial job and the number of displayed builds and save the configuration.

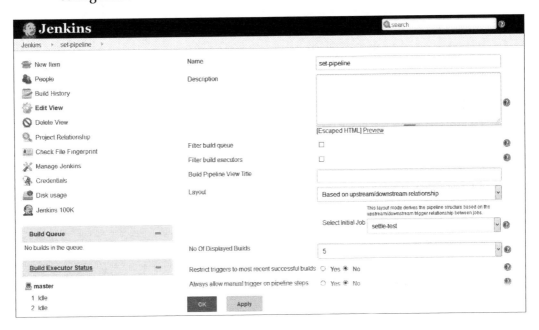

4. In a configuration of the build pipeline, select job to trigger parameterized build as `settle-build` job in **Post-build Actions**. It will be the first build job in the pipeline.

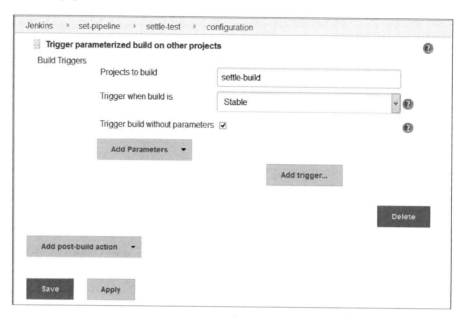

5. In a `settle-build` job, trigger the parameterized build on the `settle-aws-provisioning` job in **Post-build Actions**.

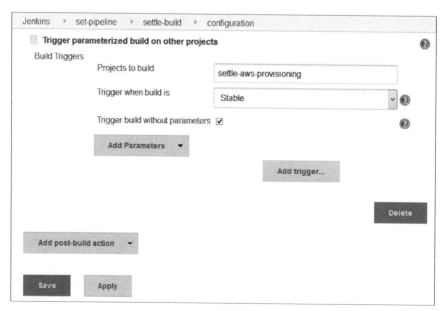

6. In a `settle-aws-provisioning` job, the manual build steps for a `settle-deploy` job in **Post-build Actions**.

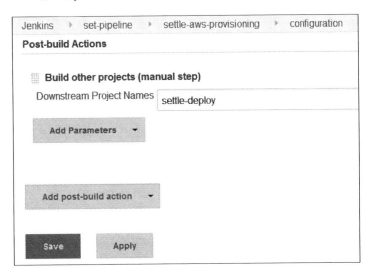

7. In a `settle-aws-provisioning` job, trigger the parameterized build on the `settle-deploy` job in **Post-build Actions**. In the `settle-deploy` build job, we can write script or execute commands so that it can deploy `war` file to newly provisioned virtual machine in the cloud environment.

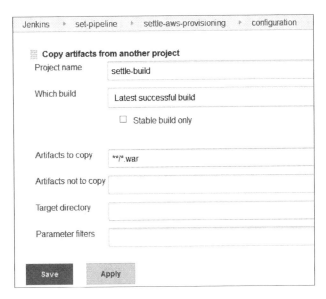

8. Go to the dashboard view, which we created earlier, and verify the pipeline created after our configuration in build jobs in the previous section. The new build pipeline will be created as shown in the following diagram:

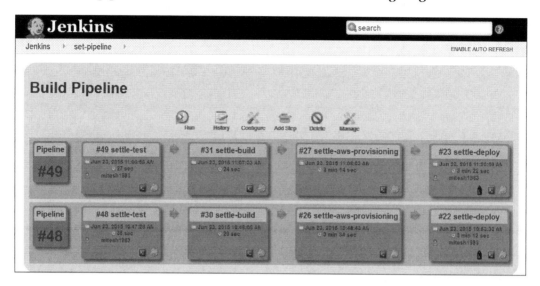

For more details, visit https://wiki.jenkins-ci.org/display/JENKINS/Build+Pipeline+Plugin.

Self-test questions

Q1. In which areas does the Extended E-mail plugin provide customization?

1. Triggers
2. Content
3. Recipients
4. All of the above

Q2. The Workspace cleanup plugin provides an option to clean the workspace when status of build is:

1. Success
2. Unstable
3. Failure
4. Not Built
5. Aborted
6. All of the above

Summary

We learned how to use some important plugins to aid the existing features of Jenkins to address specific requirements. We covered all basic usage of Jenkins, including installing runtime environment, creating build jobs, using Jenkins on Cloud, monitoring, management, security, and additional plugins. For the scope of this book, this seems sufficient. Next step is about provisioning resources dynamically in Cloud environment to achieve end to end automation in the DevOps journey.

If you want a happy ending, that depends of course on where you stop your story. We certainly know where to stop ours!

Index

T

Task Scanner plugin
 about 113
 URL 113
Tomcat
 about 68
 installing 68, 69

V

VisualSVN server
 installing, on Windows 28-36
 URL 28
VMware ESXi/vSphere Auto-Scaling plugin
 about 95
 URL 96

W

war file
 deploying, from Jenkins to Tomcat 70-76
Workflow plugin
 about 94
 URL 94
Workspace Cleanup plugin
 about 144
 installing 145
 URL 145

Thank you for buying
Jenkins Essentials

About Packt Publishing

Packt, pronounced 'packed', published its first book, *Mastering phpMyAdmin for Effective MySQL Management*, in April 2004, and subsequently continued to specialize in publishing highly focused books on specific technologies and solutions.

Our books and publications share the experiences of your fellow IT professionals in adapting and customizing today's systems, applications, and frameworks. Our solution-based books give you the knowledge and power to customize the software and technologies you're using to get the job done. Packt books are more specific and less general than the IT books you have seen in the past. Our unique business model allows us to bring you more focused information, giving you more of what you need to know, and less of what you don't.

Packt is a modern yet unique publishing company that focuses on producing quality, cutting-edge books for communities of developers, administrators, and newbies alike. For more information, please visit our website at www.packtpub.com.

About Packt Open Source

In 2010, Packt launched two new brands, Packt Open Source and Packt Enterprise, in order to continue its focus on specialization. This book is part of the Packt Open Source brand, home to books published on software built around open source licenses, and offering information to anybody from advanced developers to budding web designers. The Open Source brand also runs Packt's Open Source Royalty Scheme, by which Packt gives a royalty to each open source project about whose software a book is sold.

Writing for Packt

We welcome all inquiries from people who are interested in authoring. Book proposals should be sent to author@packtpub.com. If your book idea is still at an early stage and you would like to discuss it first before writing a formal book proposal, then please contact us; one of our commissioning editors will get in touch with you.

We're not just looking for published authors; if you have strong technical skills but no writing experience, our experienced editors can help you develop a writing career, or simply get some additional reward for your expertise.

Jenkins Continuous Integration Cookbook

Second Edition

ISBN: 978-1-78439-008-2   Paperback: 408 pages

Over 90 recipes to produce great result from Jenkins using pro-level practices, techniques, and solutions

1. Explore the use of more than 40 best-of-breed plug-ins for improving efficiency.

2. Secure and maintain Jenkins by integrating it with LDAP and CAS, which is a Single Sign-on solution.

3. Step-by-step, easy-to-use instructions to optimize the existing features of Jenkins using the complete set of plug-ins that Jenkins offers.

Apache Flume: Distributed Log Collection for Hadoop

Second Edition

ISBN: 978-1-78439-217-8   Paperback: 178 pages

Design and implement a series of Flume agents to send streamed date into Hadoop

1. Construct a series of Flume agents using the Apache Flume service to efficiently collect, aggregate, and move large amounts of event data.

2. Configure failover paths and load balancing to remove single points of failure.

3. Use this step-by-step guide to stream logs from application servers to Hadoop's HDFS.

Please check **www.PacktPub.com** for information on our titles

Apache Maven Cookbook

ISBN: 978-1-78528-612-4   Paperback: 272 pages

Over 90 hands-on recipes to successfully build and automate development life cycle tasks following Maven conventions and best practices

1. Understand the features of Apache Maven that makes it a powerful tool for build automation.

2. Full of real-world scenarios covering multi-module builds and best practices to make the most out of Maven projects.

3. A step-by-step tutorial guide full of pragmatic examples.

Learning Force.com Application Development

ISBN: 978-1-78217-279-6   Paperback: 406 pages

Use the Force.com platform to design and develop real-world, cutting-edge cloud applications

1. Design, build, and customize real-world applications on the Force.com platform.

2. Reach out to users through public websites and ensure that your Force.com application becomes popular.

3. Discover the tools that will help you develop and deploy your application.

Please check **www.PacktPub.com** for information on our titles

Made in the USA
San Bernardino, CA
15 August 2016